2nd edition © 2011 Bolchazy-Carducci Publishers, Inc.

ISBN 978-0-86516-771-1

Vocabulary Cards
and Grammatical Forms Summary for
Wheelock's Latin

WHEELOCK'S LATIN

7TH EDITION

THE CLASSIC INTRODUCTORY LATIN COURSE, BASED ON THE WRITINGS
OF CICERO, VERGIL, AND OTHER MAJOR ROMAN AUTHORS

CHAPTERS 1–20

FREDERIC M. WHEELOCK
and RICHARD A. LaFLEUR

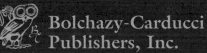

**Bolchazy-Carducci
Publishers, Inc.**

1570 Baskin Road, Mundelein, IL 60060
Phone: (847) 526-4344; *Fax:* (847) 526-2867
www.bolchazy.com

Vocabulary Cards
and Grammatical Forms Summary for
Wheelock's Latin

Vocabulary Cards
and Grammatical Forms Summary for
Wheelock's Latin

Card Storagebox Top 1

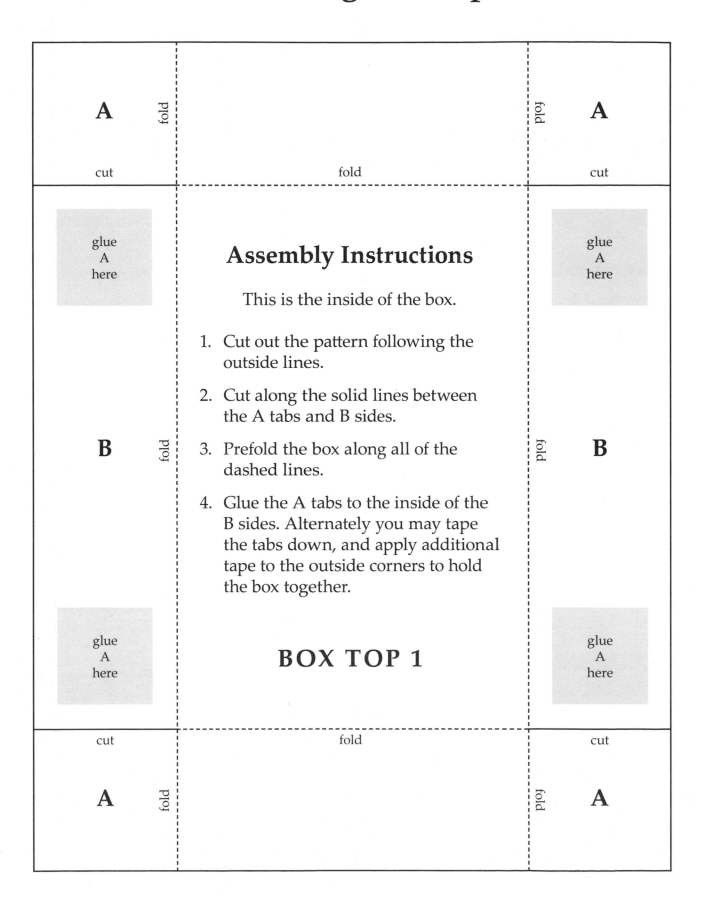

A

fold

A

fold

cut

fold

cut

glue
A
here

glue
A
here

Assembly Instructions

This is the inside of the box.

1. Cut out the pattern following the outside lines.

2. Cut along the solid lines between the A tabs and B sides.

3. Prefold the box along all of the dashed lines.

4. Glue the A tabs to the inside of the B sides. Alternately you may tape the tabs down, and apply additional tape to the outside corners to hold the box together.

B

fold

B

fold

glue
A
here

glue
A
here

BOX TOP 1

cut

fold

cut

A

fold

fold

A

2nd edition © 2011 Bolchazy-Carducci Publishers, Inc.

ISBN 978-0-86516-771-1

Vocabulary Cards
and Grammatical Forms Summary for
Wheelock's Latin

WHEELOCK'S LATIN

7TH EDITION

THE CLASSIC INTRODUCTORY LATIN COURSE, BASED ON THE WRITINGS
OF CICERO, VERGIL, AND OTHER MAJOR ROMAN AUTHORS

CHAPTERS 21–40

FREDERIC M. WHEELOCK
and RICHARD A. LAFLEUR

Vocabulary Cards
and Grammatical Forms Summary for
Wheelock's Latin

Vocabulary Cards
and Grammatical Forms Summary for
Wheelock's Latin

Bolchazy-Carducci
Publishers, Inc.
1570 Baskin Road, Mundelein, IL 60060
Phone: (847) 526-4344; *Fax:* (847) 526-2867
www.bolchazy.com

Card Storagebox Top 2

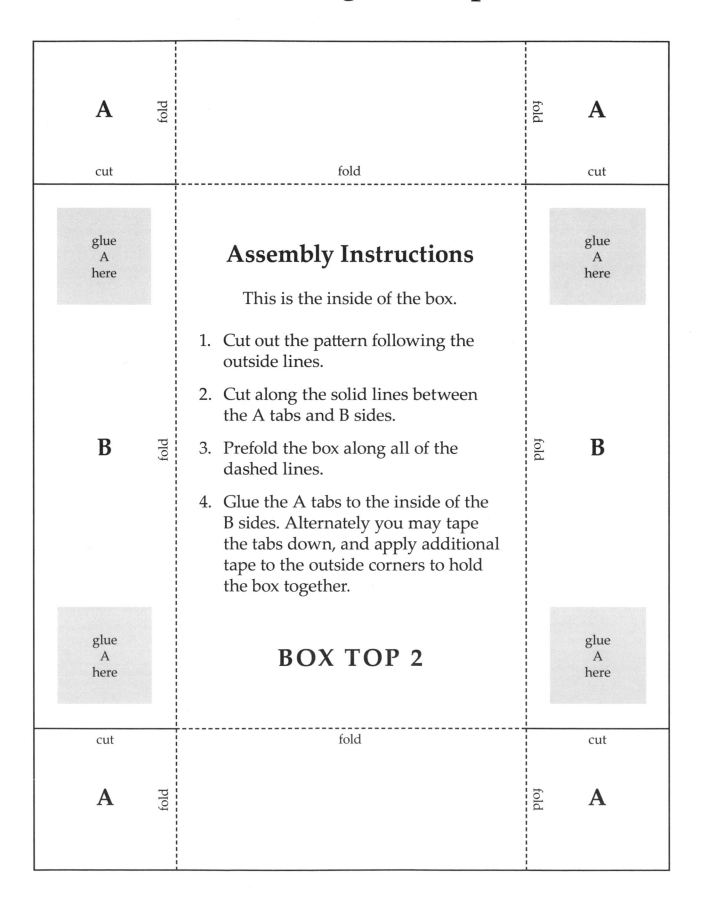

A

fold

fold

A

cut

fold

cut

glue
A
here

glue
A
here

Assembly Instructions

This is the inside of the box.

1. Cut out the pattern following the outside lines.

2. Cut along the solid lines between the A tabs and B sides.

3. Prefold the box along all of the dashed lines.

4. Glue the A tabs to the inside of the B sides. Alternately you may tape the tabs down, and apply additional tape to the outside corners to hold the box together.

B

fold

fold

B

glue
A
here

BOX TOP 2

glue
A
here

cut

fold

cut

A

fold

fold

A

VOCABULARY CARDS
AND GRAMMATICAL FORMS SUMMARY
for
WHEELOCK'S LATIN

by
RICHARD A. LAFLEUR
University of Georgia
and
Brad Tillery
North Oconee High School in Oconee County, Georgia
— SECOND EDITION —

This package contains two convenient study-aids: vocabulary cards and a summary of grammatical forms for use with the best-selling introductory Latin textbook, *Wheelock's Latin*. The form summaries, including paradigms for noun and adjective declensions, pronouns, adverbs, numerals, and regular and irregular verb conjugations, are reproduced from *Wheelock's Latin* for handy reference and inclusion in your Latin notebook.

The vocabulary cards are arranged in the same order as in *Wheelock's Latin*, chapter by chapter, and are perforated for easy separation; easily assembled boxes are included for convenient storage.

Each card contains, on one side, the full Latin vocabulary entry (with macrons, accents, and complete principal parts for verbs and nominative and genitive forms for nouns) and, on the other side, the English meanings given in Wheelock plus a selection of derivatives and cognates. The cards are numbered consecutively from 1–877, and an alphabetical list including these numbers is also provided for cross-reference.

Cards for the chapter you are currently studying, as well as for any other words you have not yet mastered, should be carried with you everywhere, in your pocket or backpack; always learn and practice vocabulary by pronouncing the words ALOUD, with careful attention to long vowels and accents; and, remembering that *repetitio est mater memoriae*, you should review and test yourself with these cards every day.

Wheelock's Latin, copyright by Martha Wheelock, Deborah Wheelock Taylor, and Richard A. LaFleur. "WHEELOCK'S" is a trademark of Martha Wheelock and Deborah Wheelock Taylor. *Wheelock's Latin*, by Frederic M. Wheelock and revised by Richard A. LaFleur, is available through your local bookstore or online at www.harpercollins.com

WHEELOCK'S LATIN IS BETTER THAN EVER! *Wheelock's Latin*, 7th Edition: a comprehensive introductory course, based on ancient authors, with self-tutorial exercises and key, extensive vocabularies and supplementary readings, numerous illustrations and maps, online audio and Teacher's Guide, in paperback and hardcover. Also available: *Workbook for Wheelock's Latin* and the intermediate textbook *Wheelock's Latin Reader*. HarperCollins Publishers, 10 East 53rd Street, New York, NY 10022; www.harpercollins.com and www.wheelockslatin.com

Bolchazy-Carducci Publishers, Inc.
Mundelein, Illinois USA
www.bolchazy.com • www.wheelockslatin.com

Editor
Laurie Haight Keenan

**Vocabulary Cards and
Grammatical Forms Summary
for Wheelock's Latin**

Richard A. LaFleur
and
Brad Tillery

— Second Edition —

Second edition © 2011 Bolchazy-Carducci Publishers, Inc.

Printed in the United States of America
2020
by Action Printing
Bolchazy-Carducci Publishers, Inc.
1570 Baskin Road
Mundelein, Illinois 60060 USA
www.bolchazy.com

ISBN 978-0-86516-771-1

mē

quid

níhil

nōn

saépe

sī

ámō, amáre, amávī, amátum

amábō tē

cógitō, cōgitáre, cōgitávī, cōgitátum

débeō, dēbére, débuī, débitum

what   me, myself

not   nothing

                                  (nihilism, annihilate)

if   often

please   to love, like

                                  (amatory, Amanda)

to owe; ought, must, should   to think, ponder, consider, plan

(debt, debit, due, duty)   (cogitate, cogitation)

dō, dáre, dédī, dátum

érrō, erráre, errávī, errátum

laúdō, laudáre, laudávī, laudátum

móneō, monére, mónuī, mónitum

sálveō, salvére

sálvē, salvéte

sérvō, serváre, servávī, servátum

cōnsérvō, cōnserváre, cōnservávī, cōnservátum

térreō, terrére, térruī, térritum

váleō, valére, váluī, valitúrum

to wander; err, go astray,
be mistaken, make a mistake

(erratic, erroneous, aberration)

to give, offer

(date, data)

to remind, advise, warn

(admonish, monitor, monument, premonition)

to praise

(laud, laudable, laudatory)

hello, greetings

to be well, be in good health

(salvation, salver, salvage)

to preserve, conserve, maintain

(conservative, conservation)

to preserve, save, keep, guard

(observe, preserve, reserve, reservoir)

to be strong, have power; be well

(valid, prevail, prevalent, valedictory)

to frighten, terrify

(terrible, terrific, terror, deter)

Chapter 1 (21)	Chapter 1 (22)
válē, valéte	vídeō, vidére, vídī, vísum
Chapter 1 (23)	Chapter 2 (24)
vócō, vocáre, vocávī, vocátum	fáma, fámae (f)
Chapter 2 (25)	Chapter 2 (26)
fórma, fórmae (f)	fortúna, fortúnae (f)
Chapter 2 (27)	Chapter 2 (28)
íra, írae (f)	naúta, naútae (m)
Chapter 2 (29)	Chapter 2 (30)
pátria, pátriae (f)	pecúnia, pecúniae (f)

to see; observe, understand

(provide, evident, view, revise)

good-bye, farewell

rumor, report; fame, reputation

(famous, defame, infamy)

to call, summon

(vocation, vocabulary, invoke, provoke)

fortune, luck

(fortunate, unfortunate)

form, shape; beauty

(formal, format, formula, deform)

sailor

(nautical)

ire, anger

(irate, irascible)

money

(pecuniary, impecunious)

fatherland, native land, (one's) country

(expatriate, repatriate)

philosóphia, philosóphiae (f)

poéna, poénae (f)

poénās dáre

poḗta, poḗtae (m)

pórta, pórtae (f)

puélla, puéllae (f)

rósa, rósae (f)

senténtia, senténtiae (f)

víta, vítae (f)

antíquus, antíqua, antíquum

penalty, punishment

(penalize, penalty, pain, subpoena)

philosophy

poet

(poetry, poetaster)

to pay the penalty

girl

gate, entrance

(portal, portico, porch, porthole)

feeling, thought, opinion, vote,
sentence

(sententious, sentencing)

rose

(rosary, roseate, rosette)

ancient, old-time

(antiquities, antiquated, antiquarian)

life; mode of life

(vital, vitality, vitamin, revitalize)

mágnus, mágna, mágnum

méus, méa, méum

múltus, múlta, múltum

túus, túa, túum

et

et . . . et

sed

Ō

síne (+abl.)

est

my   large, great; important

                                      (magnify, magnificent, magnitude)

your *(sing.)*   much, many

                                      (multitude; multiply; multi-, *prefix*)

both . . . and   and, even

O! Oh!   but

is   without

                                      (sinecure, sans)

áger, ágrī (m)

agrícola, agrícolae (m)

amíca, amícae (f)
or
amícus, amícī (m)

fémina, féminae (f)

fília, fíliae (f)

fīliábus *(dat. & abl. pl.)*

fílius, fíliī (m)

númerus, númerī (m)

pópulus, pópulī (m)

púer, púerī (m)

sapiéntia, sapiéntiae (f)

farmer

field, farm

(agrarian, agriculture, agronomy)

woman

friend

(female, feminine, femininity)

(amicable, amiable, amity)

son

daughter

(affiliation, filial)

the people, a people, a nation

number

(populace, population, popularity)

(numeral, innumerable, enumerate)

wisdom

boy;
boys, children *(pl.)*

(sapience, sapient, sage, savant)

(puerile, puerility)

vir, vírī (m)

avắrus, avắra, avắrum

paúcī, paúcae, paúca
(usually pl.)

Rōmắnus, Rōmắna, Rōmắnum

dē (+abl.)

in (+abl.)

hódiē

sémper

hábeō, habḗre, hábuī, hábitum

sátiō, satiắre, satiắvī, satiắtum

greedy, avaricious

(avarice)

man, hero

(virtue, virile, triumvirate)

Roman

(romance, romantic)

few, a few

(paucity)

in, on

(inhabit, inscribe, inspect)

down from, from; concerning, about

(de-, *prefix with meanings such as down, away, aside, out, off;* deciduous, deter, describe)

always

(sempiternal, sempre)

today

to satisfy, sate

(satiate, insatiable, satisfaction)

to have, hold, possess; consider, regard

(inhabit, habit, habitat)

bắsium, bắsiī (n)

béllum, béllī (n)

cōnsílium, cōnsíliī (n)

cúra, cúrae (f)

dốnum, dốnī (n)

exítium, exítiī (n)

magíster, magístrī (m)
or
magístra, magístrae (f)

móra, mórae (f)

níhil (n)
(indeclinable)

óculus, óculī (m)

war

(bellicose, belligerent, rebel, revel)

care, attention, caution, anxiety

(cure, curator, curious, sinecure)

destruction, ruin

(exit)

delay

(moratorium, demur)

eye

(ocular, binoculars, monocle)

kiss

plan, purpose, counsel, advice,
judgment, wisdom

(counsel, counselor)

gift, present

(donate, donation, condone)

schoolmaster, teacher, master
or
schoolmistress, teacher, mistress

(magistrate, maestro, mastery)

nothing

(nihilism, annihilate)

offícium, offíciī (n)

ótium, ótiī (n)

perículum, perículī (n)

remédium, remédiī (n)

béllus, bélla, béllum

bónus, bóna, bónum

hūmā́nus, hūmā́na, hūmā́num

málus, mála, málum

párvus, párva, párvum

stúltus, stúlta, stúltum

leisure, peace

(negotiate, otiose)

duty, service

(office, officer, official)

cure, remedy

(remedial, remediation)

danger, risk

(peril, perilous, imperil)

good, kind

(bonus, bonanza, bounty, bona fide)

pretty, handsome, charming

(belle, beauty, embellish)

bad, wicked, evil

(malicious; malign; malady; mal-, *prefix*)

pertaining to man, human; humane, kind; refined, cultivated

(humanity, humanitarian, inhuman)

foolish

(stultify, stultification)

small, little

(parvo, parvovirus)

Chapter 4	(91)	Chapter 4	(92)

stúltus, stúltī (m)

vĕrus, vĕra, vĕrum

Chapter 4 (93) Chapter 4 (94)

iúvō, iuváre, iúvī, iútum
or
ádiuvō, adiuváre, adiúvī, adiútum

sum, ésse, fúī, futúrum

Chapter 5 (95) Chapter 5 (96)

adulēscéntia, adulēscéntiae (f)

ánimus, ánimī (m)

Chapter 5 (97) Chapter 5 (98)

ánimī, animórum (m)

caélum, caélī (n)

Chapter 5 (99) Chapter 5 (100)

cúlpa, cúlpae (f)

glória, glóriae (f)

true, real, proper

(verify, very, veracity)

a fool

(stultify, stultification)

to be, exist

(essence, essential, future)

to help, aid, assist; please

(adjutant, aid)

soul, spirit, mind

(animus, animosity, unanimous)

youth, young manhood; youthfulness

(adolescence, adolescent)

sky, heaven

(ceiling, celestial, cerulean)

high spirits, pride, courage

glory, fame

(glorify, glorious)

fault, blame

(culpable, culprit, exculpate)

vérbum, vérbī (n)

tē

(abl. & acc. sing.)

líber, líbera, líberum

nóster, nóstra, nóstrum

púlcher, púlchra, púlchrum

sā́nus, sā́na, sā́num

ígitur

-ne

própter

crās

you, yourself

word

(verb, adverb, verbose, proverb)

our, ours

free

(nostrum, paternoster)

(liberal, liberality, libertine)

sound, healthy, sane

beautiful, handsome; fine

(sanity, sanitary, insane)

(pulchritude)

interrogative suffix attached to the first word of a sentence, typically the verb or another word on which the question hinges, to introduce a question whose answer is uncertain

therefore, consequently

tomorrow

on account of, because of

(procrastination)

héri

quándō

sī quándō

sátis

(indeclinable noun, adj., and adv.)

tum

cḗnō, cēnā́re, cēnā́vī, cēnā́tum

cúlpō, culpā́re, culpā́vī, culpā́tum

remáneō, remanḗre, remā́nsī, remā́nsum
or
máneō, manḗre, mā́nsī, mā́nsum

súperō, superā́re, superā́vī, superā́tum

déa, déae (f)
deā́bus *(dat. & abl. pl.)*

when

yesterday

enough, sufficient (-ly)

if ever

(satisfy, satisfactory, satiate)

then, at that time;
thereupon, in the next place

to dine

(cenacle)

to remain, stay, stay behind, abide,
continue

to blame, censure

(permanent, remnant, mansion)

(culpable, exculpate)

goddess

to be above, have the upper hand,
surpass; overcome, conquer

(superable, insuperable)

déus, déī (m)
déus *(voc. sing.)*
dī *or* déī *(nom. pl.)*
dīs *or* déīs *(dat. & abl. pl.)*

discípulus, discípulī (m)

īnsídiae, īnsidiárum (f. pl.)

líber, líbrī (m)

tyránnus, tyránnī (m)

vítium, vítiī (n)

Graécus, Graéca, Graécum

Graécus, Graécī (m)

perpétuus, perpétua, perpétuum

plénus, pléna, plénum

learner, pupil, student
(male)

(disciple, discipline)

god

(adieu, deify, deity)

book

(library, libretto)

ambush, plot, treachery

(insidious, insidiously)

fault, crime, vice

(vitiate, vicious)

absolute ruler, tyrant

(tyrannous, tyrannicide)

a Greek

Greek

full, abundant, generous

(plenary, plentiful, replenish)

perpetual, lasting, uninterrupted,
continuous

(perpetuate, perpetuity)

sálvus, sálva, sálvum

secúndus, secúnda, secúndum

véster, véstra, véstrum

-que

discípula, discípulae (f)

úbi

íbi

nunc

quā́rē

póssum, pósse, pótuī

second; favorable

(secondary, secondo)

safe, sound

(salvation, salutary)

and

(enclitic conjunction; appended to the second of two words to be joined)

your

(pl.)

where, when

(ubiquitous, ubiquity)

learner, pupil, student
(female)

(disciple, discipline)

now, at present

(quidnunc, Nunc Dimittis)

there

(alibi, ib. *or* ibid)

to be able, can, could, have power

(posse, possible, potent, potential)

because of which thing *(lit.);*
therefore, wherefore, why

Chapter 6 (141)	Chapter 7 (142)
tólerō, tolerắre, tolerắvī, tolerắtum	ámor, amóris (m)

Chapter 7 (143)	Chapter 7 (144)
cármen, cárminis (n)	cívitās, cīvitắtis (f)

Chapter 7 (145)	Chapter 7 (146)
córpus, córporis (n)	hómō, hóminis (m)

Chapter 7 (147)	Chapter 7 (148)
lábor, labóris (m)	líttera, lítterae (f)

Chapter 7 (149)	Chapter 7 (150)
lítterae, litterắrum (f. pl.)	mōs, móris (m)

love

(amorous, enamored)

to bear, endure

(tolerate, tolerable, intolerance)

state, citizenship

(citizen, city)

song, poem

(charm, charming)

human being, man

(homicide, homage, homo sapiens)

body

(corps, corpse, corporation)

a letter of the alphabet

(literal, illiterate, alliteration)

labor, work, toil;
a work, production

(laboratory, collaborate, elaborate)

habit, custom, manner

(moral, morale)

a letter (epistle), literature

(lettered, literary)

mőrēs, mőrum (m. pl.)

nőmen, nőminis (n)

pāx, pácis (f)

rēgína, rēgínae (f)

rēx, régis (m)

témpus, témporis (n)

térra, térrae (f)

úxor, uxőris (f)

vírgō, vírginis (f)

vírtūs, virtűtis (f)

name

(nomenclature, noun, ignominy, misnomer)

habits, morals, character

(mores, morality)

queen

(regina)

peace

(pacify, pacific, appease)

time; occasion, opportunity

(temporary, temporal, tense)

king

(regal, regalia, regicide, royal)

wife

(uxorial, uxorious)

earth, ground, land, country

(terrestrial, terrace, territory)

manliness, courage; excellence,
character, worth, virtue

(virtuoso, virtuosity, virtual)

maiden, virgin

(virginal)

nóvus, nóva, nóvum

post (+acc.)

sub (+abl., *with verbs of rest*)
or
sub (+acc., *with verbs of motion*)

aúdeō, audére, aúsus sum

nécō, necáre, necávī, necátum

Cícerō, Cicerónis (m)

cópia, cópiae (f)

cópiae, cōpiárum (f. pl.)

fráter, frátris (m)

laus, laúdis (f)

after, behind

(posterity; post-, *prefix*)

new; strange

(novel, novice, innovate)

to dare

(audacious, audacity)

under, up under, close to,
down to/into, to/at the foot of

(sub-, suc-, suf-, sug-, sup-, sus-, *prefixes*)

(Marcus Tullius) Cicero

to murder, kill

(internecine)

supplies, troops, forces

abundance, supply

(copious, copy, cornucopia)

praise, glory, fame

(laud, laudable, magna cum laude)

brother

(fraternal, fraternity, fraternize)

lībértās, lībertátis (f)

rátiō, ratiónis (f)

scríptor, scrīptóris (m)

sóror, soróris (f)

victória, victóriae (f)

dum

ad (+acc.)

ex *or* ē (+abl.)

ex *(before consonants or vowels)*

ē *(before consonants only)*

númquam

támen

reckoning, account; reason, judgment,
consideration; system; manner,
method

(ratio, ration, rational)

liberty

(libertarian, libertarianism)

sister

(sorority)

writer, author

(scriptorium)

while, as long as, at the same time that;
or
until *(+subjunctive)*

victory

(victorious)

out of, from, from within;
by reason of, on account of;
of *(following cardinal numerals)*

(ex-, e-, ef-, *prefixes;* exact, event, effect)

to, up to, near to

(ad-, ac-, ap-, a-, *prefixes;*
admonish, accept, appellation, aspect)

nevertheless, still

never

ágō, ágere, égī, áctum

grátiās ágere (+dat.)

dēmőnstrō, dēmōnstráre, dēmōnstrávī, dēmōnstrátum

díscō, díscere, dídicī

dóceō, docḗre, dócuī, dóctum

dū́cō, dū́cere, dū́xī, dúctum

gérō, gérere, géssī, géstum

scrī́bō, scrī́bere, scrī́psī, scrī́ptum

tráhō, tráhere, trā́xī, tráctum

víncō, víncere, vī́cī, víctum

to thank someone;
to give thanks to

to drive, lead, do, act;
pass, spend *(life or time)*

(agent, agenda, agile, active, actor)

to learn

to point out, show, demonstrate

(discipline, disciple)

(demonstration, demonstrative)

to lead; consider, regard; prolong

to teach

(ductile, abduct, produce, reduce)

(docile, document, doctor, doctrine)

to write, compose

to carry; carry on, manage, conduct,
wage, accomplish, perform

(describe, inscribe, postscript, scripture)

(gesture, belligerent, suggest, register)

to conquer, overcome

to draw, drag; derive, acquire

(convince, convict, evict, victor)

(attract, contract, tractor)

lócus, lócī (m)

lóca, locṓrum (n. pl.)

lócī, locṓrum (m. pl.)

mórbus, mórbī (m)

stúdium, stúdiī (n)

hic, haec, hoc

ílle, ílla, íllud

íste, ísta, ístud

álius, ália, áliud

áliī . . . áliī

places, region

place; passage in literature

(allocate, dislocate, locality)

disease, sickness

passages in literature

(morbid, morbidity)

this; the latter;
he, she, it, they

eagerness, zeal, pursuit, study

(ad hoc)

(studio, studious)

that of yours, that;
such (as you have, as you speak of);
sometimes with contemptuous force, e.g.,
that despicable, that wretched

that; the former; the famous;
he, she, it, they

some . . . others

other, another

(alias, alibi, alien)

álter, áltera, álterum

neúter, neútra, neútrum

núllus, núlla, núllum

sólus, sóla, sólum

nōn sólum . . . sed étiam

tótus, tóta, tótum

úllus, úlla, úllum

únus, úna, únum

úter, útra, útrum

énim

not either, neither

(neutrality, neutron)

the other (of two), second

(alter, alteration, alternative)

alone, only, the only

(solitary, soliloquy, solo, desolate)

not any, no, none

(null, nullify, annul)

whole, entire

(total, totality)

not only . . . but also

one, single, alone

(unit, unite, union, uniform)

any

for, in fact, truly

either, which (of two)

Chapter 9	(211)	Chapter 9	(212)
in (+acc.)		nímis *or* nímium	

Chapter 10	(213)	Chapter 10	(214)
amīcítia, amīcítiae (f)		cupíditās, cupiditátis (f)	

Chapter 10	(215)	Chapter 10	(216)
hőra, hőrae (f)		nātűra, nātűrae (f)	

Chapter 10	(217)	Chapter 10	(218)
senéctūs, senectűtis (f)		tímor, timőris (m)	

Chapter 10	(219)	Chapter 10	(220)
vĕritās, vēritátis (f)		vía, víae (f)	

too, too much, excessively;
(in a positive sense, esp. with adjectives and adverbs) exceedingly, very

into, toward; against

(in-, il-, ir-, im-, *prefixes;*
induct, illusion, imminent)

desire, longing, passion; cupidity, avarice

(concupiscence, Cupid)

friendship

(amicable, amity)

nature

(natural, preternatural, supernatural)

hour, time

(horologe)

fear

(timorous, timorousness)

old age

(senile, senility)

way, road, street

(viaduct, deviate, devious, trivial)

truth

(verify, veritable, verity)

volúptās, voluptátis (f)

beátus, beáta, beátum

quóniam

cum (+abl.)

aúdiō, audíre, audívī, audítum

cápiō, cápere, cépī, cáptum

dícō, dícere, díxī, díctum

fáciō, fácere, fécī, fáctum

fúgiō, fúgere, fúgī, fugitúrum

véniō, veníre, vénī, véntum

happy, fortunate, blessed

(beatify, beatitude)

pleasure

(voluptuary, voluptuous)

with

(com-, con-, cor-, col-, co-, *prefixes;*
collect, commit, connect, cooperate, correct)

since, inasmuch as

to take, capture, seize, get

(capable, capsule, captive, captor)

to hear, listen to

(audible, audience, audition)

to make, do, accomplish

(facile, fact, faculty, feasible)

to say, tell, speak; name, call

(dictate, dictionary, contradict, verdict)

to come

(advent, adventure, convene, event)

to flee, hurry away, escape;
go into exile; avoid, shun

(fugitive, centrifugal, refuge)

invéniō, invenīre, invḗnī, invéntum

vívō, vívere, víxī, víctum

cáput, cápitis (n)

cṓnsul, cṓnsulis (m)

nḗmō, nūllī́us, nḗminī, nḗminem,
nū́llō *or* nū́llā (m *or* f)

égo
and
nōs

tū
and
vōs

is, éa, id

ídem, éadem, ídem

amī́cus, amī́ca, amī́cum

to live

(revive, survive, vivid)

to come upon, find

(invent, inventory)

consul

(consular, consulate)

head; leader; beginning; life;
heading; chapter

(capitol, capitulate, captain, cadet)

I
and
we

(ego, egotism, egotistical)

no one, nobody

this, that; he, she, it

(id, id est)

you

friendly

(amicable, amiable)

the same

(idem, identical, identity, identify)

cắrus, cắra, cắrum

quod

néque *or* nec

néque . . . néque *or* nec . . . nec

aútem

béne

étiam

intéllegō, intellégere, intelléxī, intelléctum

míttō, míttere, mísī, míssum

séntiō, sentíre, sénsī, sénsum

because

dear

(caress, charity, cherish)

neither . . . nor

and not, nor

well, satisfactorily, quite

however; moreover

(benediction, benefit, benevolent)

to understand

even, also

(intelligent, intellect, intellectual)

to feel, perceive, think, experience

to send, let go

(consent, dissent, resent, sentimental)

(admit, commit, promise, transmit)

aduléscēns, adulēscéntis (m *and* f)

ánnus, ánnī (m)

Ásia, Ásiae (f)

Caésar, Caésaris (m)

máter, mátris (f)

médicus, médicī (m)
and
médica, médicae (f)

páter, pátris (m)

patiéntia, patiéntiae (f)

prīncípium, prīncípiī (n)

acérbus, acérba, acérbum

year

(annual, anniversary, perennial)

young man, young woman

(adolescent, adult)

Caesar

(kaiser, czar, tsar, caesarean)

Asia

doctor, physician

(medical, medicine)

mother

(maternal, matrimony, matriculate)

suffering; patience, endurance

(patient, impatient)

father

(paternal, patrician, patronage)

harsh, bitter, grievous

(acerbity, exacerbate)

beginning

(principal, principle)

prō (+abl.)

díū

núper

āmíttō, āmíttere, āmī́sī, āmíssum

cádō, cádere, cécidī, cāsū́rum

créō, creā́re, creā́vī, creā́tum

dīvítiae, dīvitiā́rum (f. pl.)

fáctum, fáctī (n)

sígnum, sígnī (n)

ípse, ípsa, ípsum

long, for a long time

in front of, before, on behalf of,
for the sake of, in return for,
instead of, for, as

(pro-, *prefix*)

to send away; lose, let go

recently

to create

to fall

(creation, creativity, creature)

(cadence, case, cascade, accident)

deed, act, achievement

riches, wealth

(fact, faction, feat)

myself, yourself, himself, herself,
itself, themselves, the very, the actual

sign, signal, indication; seal

(ipso facto)

(assign, consign, design, insignia)

quísque, quídque
(cuiúsque, *gen.*; cuíque, *dat.*)

súī

dóctus, dócta, dóctum

fortūnátus, fortūnáta, fortūnátum

súus, súa, súum

nam

ánte (+acc.)

per (+acc.)

ṓlim

álō, álere, áluī, áltum

himself, herself, itself, themselves

(suicide, sui generis)

each one, each person, each thing

lucky, fortunate, happy

(unfortunate)

taught, learned, skilled

(doctor, doctorate, doctrine)

for

his own, her own, its own, their own

through; by *(with reflexive pronoun);*
thoroughly, very *(as a prefix)*

(per diem, per-, *prefix;* perfect; perhaps)

before *(in place or time)*, in front of;
before, previously *(adv.)*

(antebellum, antedate, anterior)

to nourish, support, sustain,
increase; cherish

(aliment, alimentary, alimony)

once (upon a time), long ago, formerly;
some day, in the future

dī́ligō, dīlígere, dīléxī, dīléctum

iúngō, iúngere, iúnxī, iúnctum

stō, stáre, stétī, státum

ánimal, animā́lis (n)

áqua, áquae (f)

ars, ártis (f)

aúris, aúris (f)

cī́vis, cī́vis (m *or* f)

iūs, iū́ris (n)

máre, máris (n)

to join

(joint, junction, injunction)

to esteem, love

(diligent, diligence)

a living creature, animal

(animate, animalistic)

to stand, stand still, stand firm

(stable, station, statue, establish)

art, skill

(artifact, artificial, artist, artisan)

water

(aquatic, aquarium, aqueduct)

citizen

(civil, civilian, civilize, civic)

ear

(aural, auricular)

sea

(marine, mariner, submarine)

right, justice, law

(jurisdiction, juror, jury, injury)

mors, mórtis (f)

nū́bēs, nū́bis (f)

ōs, óris (n)

pars, pártis (f)

Rṓma, Rṓmae (f)

túrba, túrbae (f)

urbs, úrbis (f)

vīs, vīs (f)

vī́rēs, vī́rium (f. pl.)

ab *or* ā (+abl.)

ab *(before consonants or vowels)*

ā *(before consonants only)*

cloud

death

(mortal, mortify, mortgage)

part, share; direction

mouth, face

(party, partial, participate, depart)

(oral, orifice)

uproar, disturbance; mob, crowd, multitude

Rome

(turbulent, disturb, perturb, trouble)

(romance, romantic)

force, power, violence

city

(violate, violent)

(urban, urbane, suburb)

away from, from; by

strength

(ab-, *prefix;* aberrant, absent, abstain)

Chapter 14 (301)	Chapter 14 (302)
trāns (+acc.)	appéllō, appelláre, appellávī, appellátum
Chapter 14 (303)	Chapter 14 (304)
cúrrō, cúrrere, cucúrrī, cúrsum	mū́tō, mūtáre, mūtávī, mūtátum
Chapter 14 (305)	Chapter 14 (306)
téneō, tenére, ténuī, téntum	vítō, vītáre, vītávī, vītátum
Chapter 15 (307)	Chapter 15 (308)
Itália, Itáliae (f)	memória, memóriae (f)
Chapter 15 (309)	Chapter 15 (310)
tempéstās, tempestátis (f)	céntum

to speak to, address (as), call, name

(appellation, appeal, appellate)

across

(transport, transmit)

to change, alter; exchange

(mutable, mutual, commute, permutation)

to run, rush, move quickly

(current, course, occur)

to avoid, shun

(inevitable)

to hold, keep, possess; restrain

(tenacious, tenure, tentacle, detain)

memory, recollection

(memoir, memorial, memorize)

Italy

(italics, italicize)

a hundred

(cent, centennial, centimeter, century)

period of time, season; weather, storm

(tempest, tempestuous)

mílle

mília, mílium (n. pl.)

míser, mísera, míserum

ínter (+acc.)

ítaque

commíttō, commíttere, commísī, commíssum

exspéctō, exspectáre, exspectávī, exspectátum

iáciō, iácere, iḗcī, iáctum

tímeō, timḗre, tímuī

únus, úna, únum

thousands

thousand

(millennium, mile, millimeter, million)

between, among

wretched, miserable, unfortunate

(intern; internal; inter-, *prefix;* international)

(misery, commiserate)

to entrust, commit

and so, therefore

(committee, commission, commitment)

to throw, hurl

to look for, expect, await

(abject, dejected, eject, object, project)

(expectancy, expectation)

one

to fear, be afraid (of)

(unite, unity, unify)

(timid, intimidate)

dúo, dúae, dúo

trēs, tría

quáttuor

quínque

sex

séptem

óctō

nóvem

décem

úndecim

three

(trio, triple, triangle)

two

(dual, duel, duo)

five

(quinquennium, quinquennial)

four

(quatrain, quattrocento, quaternary)

seven

(September, septennial, septet)

six

(sexennial, sexpartite)

nine

(November, novena)

eight

(octant, octet, October)

eleven

ten

(December, decade, decennial)

duódecim

trédecim

quattuórdecim

quíndecim

sédecim

septéndecim

duodēvīgíntī

ūndēvīgíntī

vīgíntī

vīgíntī únus
or
únus et vīgíntī

thirteen	twelve
	(duodenum)
fifteen	fourteen
seventeen	sixteen
nineteen	eighteen
twenty-one	twenty

vīgíntī dúo

or

dúo et vīgíntī

vīgíntī trēs

or

trēs et vīgíntī

vīgíntī quáttuor

or

quáttuor et vīgíntī

vīgíntī quínque

or

quínque et vīgíntī

prímus, príma, prímum

secúndus, secúnda, secúndum

tértius, tértia, tértium

quártus, quárta, quártum

quíntus, quínta, quíntum

séxtus, séxta, séxtum

twenty-three

twenty-two

twenty-five

twenty-four

second

(secondary, secondo)

first

(prime, primary, prima facie)

fourth

(quart, quarter, quartet)

third

(tertial, tertian, tertiary)

sixth

(sextant, sextet, sextuplet)

fifth

(quintet, quintuplet)

séptimus, séptima, séptimum

octávus, octáva, octávum

nőnus, nőna, nőnum

décimus, décima, décimum

ūndécimus, ūndécima, ūndécimum

duodécimus, duodécima, duodécimum

aétās, aetắtis (f)

audítor, audītőris (m)

clēméntia, clēméntiae (f)

mēns, méntis (f)

eighth

(octave, octavo)

seventh

tenth

(decimal, decimate)

ninth

(nonagenarian, nonagon)

twelfth

(duodecimal, duodecimo)

eleventh

hearer, listener,
member of an audience

(auditor, auditory, auditorium)

period of life, life, age, an age, time

(eternal, eternity)

mind, thought, intention

(mental, mentality, mention)

mildness, gentleness, mercy

(clemency, inclement)

sátura, sáturae (f)

ácer, ácris, ácre

brévis, bréve

céler, céleris, célere

diffícilis, diffícile

dúlcis, dúlce

fácilis, fácile

fórtis, fórte

íngēns, *gen.* ingéntis

iūcúndus, iūcúnda, iūcúndum

sharp, keen, eager; severe, fierce

(acrid, acrimony, eager)

satire

(satirist, satirical)

swift, quick, rapid

(celerity, accelerate)

short, small, brief

(brevity, abbreviate, abridge)

sweet; pleasant, agreeable

(dulcify, dulcet, dulcimer)

hard, difficult, troublesome

(difficulty)

strong, brave

(fort, fortify, fortitude, comfort)

easy; agreeable

(facility, facilitate)

pleasant, delightful, agreeable,
pleasing

(jocund)

huge

lóngus, lónga, lóngum

ómnis, ómne

pótēns, *gen.* poténtis

sénex, *gen.* sénis

(adj. and noun)

quam

régō, régere, réxī, réctum

libéllus, libéllī (m)

quī, quae, quod

caécus, caéca, caécum

lévis, léve

every, all

(omnibus, omnipotent, omnivorous)

long

(longitude, longevity, prolong)

old, aged *(adj.)*
or
old man *(noun)*

(senate, senator, senile, senior)

able, powerful, mighty, strong

(potent, impotent, omnipotent)

to rule, guide, direct

(regent, regime, regular, direction)

how

who, which, what, that

(quibble, quorum, sine qua non)

little book

(libel, libelous)

light; easy; slight, trivial

(levity, lever, elevate, relevant)

blind

(caecilian)

aut

aut . . . aut

cíto

quóque

admíttō, admíttere, admḗsī, admíssum

coépī, coepísse, coéptum

cúpiō, cúpere, cupívī, cupítum

déleō, dēlḗre, dēlḗvī, dēlḗtum

dēsíderō, dēsīderā́re, dēsīderā́vī,
dēsīderā́tum

incípiō, incípere, incḗpī, incéptum

either . . . or   or

also, too   quickly

                                                   (excite, incite, recite)

began   to admit, receive, let in

                                                   (admission, admissible, admittedly)

to destroy, wipe out, erase   to desire, wish, long for

(delete, indelible)   (cupidity, covet)

to begin   to desire, long for, miss

(incipient, inception)   (desire, desirous)

Chapter 17 (391)	Chapter 17 (392)
nǎvigō, nāvigǎre, nāvigǎvī, nāvigǎtum	néglegō, neglégere, negléxī, negléctum

Chapter 17 (393)	Chapter 18 (394)
récitō, recitǎre, recitǎvī, recitǎtum	flǔmen, flǔminis (n)

Chapter 18 (395)	Chapter 18 (396)
génus, géneris (n)	hóstis, hóstis (m)

Chapter 18 (397)	Chapter 18 (398)
hóstēs, hóstium (m)	lǔdus, lǔdī (m)

Chapter 18 (399)	Chapter 18 (400)
próbitās, probitǎtis (f)	sciéntia, sciéntiae (f)

to neglect, disregard

(negligent, negligible)

to sail, navigate

(navigation, navigable)

river

(flume)

to read aloud, recite

(recital, recitation)

an enemy *(of the state)*

(hostile, hostility, host)

origin; kind, type, sort, class

(genus, generic, gender, genre)

game, sport; school

(ludicrous, delude, elude, illusion)

the enemy

knowledge

(science, scientific)

uprightness, honesty

(probity, improbity)

Chapter 18   (401)   Chapter 18   (402)

clắrus, clắra, clắrum   mortắlis, mortắle

Chapter 18   (403)   Chapter 18   (404)

cūr   deínde

Chapter 18   (405)   Chapter 18   (406)

flúō, flúere, flúxī, flúxum   légō, légere, légī, léctum

Chapter 18   (407)   Chapter 18   (408)

mísceō, miscére, míscuī, míxtum   móveō, movére, mốvī, mốtum

Chapter 18   (409)   Chapter 19   (410)

vídeor, vidếrī, vísus sum   argūméntum, argūméntī (n)

mortal

(mortality, immortality)

clear, bright;
renowned, famous, illustrious

(clarify, clarity, declare)

thereupon, next, then

why

to pick out, choose; read

(elect, elegant, lecture, intellect)

to flow

(fluid, fluent, influx, affluence)

to move; arouse, affect

(mobile, motion, motor, emotion)

to mix, stir up, disturb

(miscellaneous, meddle, medley)

proof, evidence, argument

(argumentative, argumentation)

to be seen, seem, appear

aúctor, auctőris (m)

benefícium, benefíciī (n)

família, famíliae (f)

Graécia, Graéciae (f)

iŭdex, iŭdicis (m)

iūdícium, iūdíciī (n)

scélus, scéleris (n)

quis? quid?

quī? quae? quod?

cértus, cérta, cértum

benefit, kindness; favor

(beneficial, beneficiary)

increaser; author, originator

(authority, authorize)

Greece

household, family

(familial, familiar, familiarity)

judgment, decision, opinion; trial

(judicial, judicious, prejudice)

judge, juror

(judge, judgment)

who? whose? whom? what? which?

(quid pro quo, quiddity, quidnunc)

evil deed, crime, sin, wickedness

what? which? what kind of?;
(sometimes with exclamatory force)
what (a)! what sort of!

definite, sure, certain, reliable

(certify, certificate)

(cui bono)

grávis, gráve

immortális, immortále

at

nísi

cóntrā (+acc.)

iam

dēléctō, dēlectáre, dēlectávī, dēlectátum

líberō, līberáre, līberávī, līberátum

párō, paráre, parávī, parátum

coniūrátī, coniūrātórum (m)

not subject to death, immortal

(immortality, immortalize)

heavy, weighty; serious, important;
severe, grievous

if . . . not, unless; except

(nisi, nisi prius)

but; but, mind you; but, you say

now, already, soon

against

(contradict, contrast, contrary)

to free, liberate

(liberate, liberal, deliver)

to delight, charm, please

(delectable, delectation)

conspirators

(conjure, conjurer)

to prepare, provide; get, obtain

(compare, parachute, repair, separate)

córnū, córnūs (n)

frűctus, frűctūs (m)

génū, génūs (n)

mánus, mánūs (f)

métus, métūs (m)

mōns, móntis (m)

senắtus, senắtūs (m)

sénsus, sénsūs (m)

sérvitūs, servitűtis (f)

spíritus, spíritūs (m)

fruit; profit, benefit, enjoyment

(fructose, frugal)

horn

(cornea, corner, unicorn)

hand; handwriting; band

(manual, manuscript, emancipate)

knee

(genuflect, genuflection)

mountain

(mount, paramount, tantamount)

fear, dread, anxiety

(meticulous)

feeling, sense

(sensation, sensual, sensitive)

senate

(senator, senatorial)

breath, breathing; spirit, soul

(spiritual, inspire, expire)

servitude, slavery

vérsus, vérsūs (m)

commúnis, commúne

déxter, déxtra, déxtrum

siníster, sinístra, sinístrum

cáreō, carḗre, cáruī, caritū́rum
(+abl. of separation)

dēféndō, dēféndere, dēféndī,
dēfénsum

discḗdō, discḗdere, discéssī, discéssum

ṓdī, ōdísse, ōsū́rum

prohíbeō, prohibḗre, prohíbuī,
prohíbitum

prōnúntiō, prōnūntiā́re, prōnūntiā́vī,
prōnūntiā́tum

common, general,
of / for the community

(communal, communicate, communism)

line of verse

(versify, versification)

left, left-hand; harmful, ill-omened

(sinister, sinistrodextral, sinistrous)

right, right-hand

(dexterity, ambidextrous)

to ward off; defend, protect

(defendant, defense)

to be without, be deprived of, want,
lack; be free from

(caret)

to hate

(odious, odium)

to go away, depart

to proclaim, announce;
declaim; pronounce

(pronunciamento, pronunciation)

to keep (back), prevent, hinder,
restrain, prohibit

(prohibitive, prohibition)

cása, cásae (f)

caúsa, caúsae (f)

caúsā

(abl. with a preceding gen.)

fenéstra, fenéstrae (f)

fínis, fínis (m)

fínēs, fínium (m)

gēns, géntis (f)

múndus, múndī (m)

nắvis, nắvis (f)

sálūs, salútis (f)

cause, reason; case, situation

(accuse, because, excuse)

house, cottage, hut

(Casablanca, casino)

window

(defenestration, fenestrated)

for the sake of, on account of

boundaries, territory

end, limit, boundary; purpose

(affinity, define, finish, infinite)

world, universe

(mundane)

clan, race, nation, people

(gentile, gentle, gentry)

health, safety; greeting

(salutary, salutation, salute)

ship, boat

(naval, navy, navigate)

Trŏia, Trŏiae (f)

vīcínus, vīcíni (m)
and
vīcína, vīcínae (f)

vúlgus, vúlgī (n *or* m)

ásper, áspera, ásperum

átque *or* ac

íterum

contíneō, continére, contínuī,
conténtum

iúbeō, iubére, iússī, iússum

labŏrō, labōrắre, labōrắvī, labōrắtum

rápiō, rápere, rápuī, ráptum

neighbor	Troy
(vicinage, vicinal, vicinity)	
rough, harsh	the common people, mob, rabble
(exasperate, exasperation)	(vulgar, vulgate, divulge)
again, a second time	and also, and even, and in fact
(iterative, reiterate)	
to bid, order, command	to hold together, contain, keep, enclose, restrain
(jube, jussive)	(content, continual, countenance)
to seize, snatch, carry away	to labor; be in distress
(rapid, rapture, ravage, ravine)	(laboratory, laborer)

relínquō, relínquere, relíquī, relíctum

scíō, scíre, scívī, scítum

tángō, tángere, tétigī, tāctum

díēs, diḗī (m)

férrum, férrī (n)

fídēs, fídeī (f)

ígnis, ígnis (m)

módus, módī (m)

rēs, réī (f)

rēs pū́blica, réī pū́blicae (f)

to know

(science, conscience, prescience)

to leave behind, leave, abandon, desert

(relinquish, relict, delinquent)

day

(diary, journal, meridian)

to touch

(tangent, tangible, tactile, contact)

faith, trust, trustworthiness, fidelity;
promise, guarantee, protection

(confide, diffident, infidel, perfidy)

iron; sword

(ferric, farrier)

measure, bound, limit;
manner, method, mode, way

(model, moderate, modern, modest)

fire

(igneous, ignite, ignition)

state, commonwealth, republic

(republican, republicanism)

thing, matter, property, business,
affair

(real, realistic, reality)

spēs, spéī (f)

aéquus, aéqua, aéquum

fēlīx, *gen.* fēlīcis

incértus, incérta, incértum

Latínus, Latína, Latínum

médius, média, médium

quóndam

últrā (adv. *and* prep. +acc.)

prótinus

cérnō, cérnere, crévī, crétum

level, even; calm;
equal, just; favorable

(equation, equator, equinox, equivalent)

hope

(despair, desperate)

uncertain, unsure, doubtful

(incertitude)

lucky, fortunate, happy

(felicity, felicitous)

middle; the middle of

(mediterranean, median, meridian)

Latin

(Latinist, Latinity, Latino)

on the other side, beyond

(ultra, ultrasound, outrage)

formerly, once

to distinguish, discern, perceive

(discern, discreet, discretion)

immediately

ērípiō, ērípere, ērípuī, ēréptum

ínquit

tóllō, tóllere, sústulī, sublátum

arx, árcis (f)

dux, dúcis (m)

équus, équī (m)

hásta, hástae (f)

ínsula, ínsulae (f)

lítus, lítoris (n)

míles, mílitis (m)

he says *or* said

to snatch away, take away; rescue

(erepsin)

citadel, stronghold

to raise, lift up;
take away, remove, destroy

(extol, extollment, sublate)

horse

(equestrian, equine)

leader, guide;
commander, general

(duke, duchess, doge)

island

(insular, isolate, peninsula)

spear

(hastate)

soldier

(military, militant, militia)

shore, coast

(littoral)

ōrắtor, ōrātṓris (m)

sacérdōs, sacerdṓtis (m)

áliquis, áliquid

quísquis, quídquid

magnánimus, magnánima,
magnánimum

úmquam

ḗducō, ēducắre, ēducắvī, ēducắtum

gaúdeō, gaudḗre, gāvī́sus sum

osténdō, osténdere, osténdī, osténtum

pétō, pétere, petī́vī, petī́tum

priest

(sacerdotal)

orator, speaker

(oratory, oratorio)

whoever, whatever

someone, somebody, something

ever, at any time

great-hearted, brave, magnanimous

(magnanimity, magnanimously)

to be glad, rejoice

(gaud, gaudy, gaudeamus)

to bring up, educate

(education, educator)

to seek, aim at, beg, beseech

(appetite, compete, petition, repeat)

to exhibit, show, display

(ostentatious, ostensible)

Chapter 23 (511)	Chapter 23 (512)
prémō, prémere, préssī, préssum	ópprimō, opprímere, oppréssī, oppréssum
Chapter 23 (513)	Chapter 23 (514)
vértō, vértere, vértī, vérsum	āvértō, āvértere, āvértī, āvérsum
Chapter 23 (515)	Chapter 24 (516)
revértō, revértere, revértī, revérsum	Carthā́gō, Carthā́ginis (f)
Chapter 24 (517)	Chapter 24 (518)
fā́bula, fā́bulae (f)	imperátor, imperātṓris (m)
Chapter 24 (519)	Chapter 24 (520)
impérium, impériī (n)	perfúgium, perfúgiī (n)

to suppress, overwhelm,
overpower, check

(oppress, oppression)

to press; press hard, pursue

(compress, depress, express, print)

to turn away, avert

(averse, aversion)

to turn; change

(verse, version, transverse)

Carthage

to turn back

(revert, reverse, reversion)

general, commander-in-chief, emperor

(imperative)

story, tale; play

(fable, fabulous)

refuge, shelter

power to command, supreme power,
authority, command, control

(imperial, imperious, empire)

sérvus, sérvī (m)

or

sérva, sérvae (f)

sōlǽcium, sōlǽciī (n)

vúlnus, vúlneris (n)

re- *or* red-

(prefix)

ut

(+ indicative)

pósteā

accípiō, accípere, accḗpī, accéptum

excípiō, excípere, excḗpī, excéptum

recípiō, recípere, recḗpī, recéptum

péllō, péllere, pépulī, púlsum

comfort, relief

(solace, consolation, inconsolable)

slave

(serf, servant, servile, service)

again, back

(recede, remit, repeat)

wound

(vulnerable, invulnerable)

afterwards

as, just as, when

to take out, except;
take, receive, capture

(exception, exceptionable)

to take *(to one's self)*, receive, accept

to strike, push; drive out, banish

(compel, dispel, expel, repel, pulse)

to take back, regain; admit, receive

(recipe, receipt, reception)

expéllō, expéllere, éxpulī, expúlsum

nā́rrō, nārrā́re, nārrā́vī, nārrā́tum

quaérō, quaérere, quaesī́vī, quaesī́tum

rī́deō, rīdḗre, rī́sī, rī́sum

língua, línguae (f)

férōx, *gen.* ferṓcis

fidḗlis, fidḗle

géminus, gémina, géminum

sápiēns, *gen.* sapiéntis

últimus, última, últimum

to tell, report, narrate

(narration, narrative, narrator)

to drive out, expel, banish

(expellent, expulsion, expulsive)

to laugh, laugh at

(deride, derisive, ridicule, ridiculous)

to seek, look for, strive for;
ask, inquire, inquire into

(acquire, inquire, question, request)

fierce, savage

(ferocious, ferocity)

tongue; language

(linguist, linguistics, bilingual)

twin

(geminate, Gemini)

faithful, loyal

(fidelity, infidelity, infidel)

farthest, extreme; last, final

(ultimate, ultimatum)

wise, judicious *(adj.)*
and
a wise man/woman, philosopher *(noun)*

(sapiens, insipid, savant)

déhinc

hīc

áit, áiunt

crédō, crédere, crédidī, créditum
(+acc. *or* dat.)

iáceō, iacére, iácuī

négō, negáre, negávī, negátum

nésciō, nescíre, nescívī, nescítum

núntiō, nūntiáre, nūntiávī, nūntiátum

patefáciō, patefácere, patefécī,
patefáctum

pútō, putáre, putávī, putátum

here

then, next

to believe, trust

he says, they say, assert

(credence, incredible, credit)

(adage)

to deny, say that . . . not

to lie; lie prostrate; lie dead

(negate, negative, denial)

(adjacent, joist)

to announce, report, relate

to not know, be ignorant

(denounce, pronounce, renounce)

(nescient)

to reckon, suppose, judge,
think, imagine

to make open, open;
disclose, expose

(compute, dispute, amputate)

Chapter 25	(551)	Chapter 25	(552)

spḗrō, spērā́re, spērā́vī, spērā́tum

suscípiō, suscípere, suscḗpī, suscéptum

Chapter 26	(553)	Chapter 26	(554)

cḗna, cḗnae (f)

fórum, fórī (n)

Chapter 26	(555)	Chapter 26	(556)

lēx, lḗgis (f)

lī́men, lī́minis (n)

Chapter 26	(557)	Chapter 26	(558)

lūx, lúcis (f)

ménsa, ménsae (f)

Chapter 26	(559)	Chapter 26	(560)

ménsa secúnda

nox, nóctis (f)

to undertake

(susceptance, susceptible)

to hope for, hope

(despair, desperate, desperation)

marketplace, forum

(forensic)

dinner

(cenacle)

threshold

(subliminal, eliminate, preliminary)

law, statute

(legal, legislature, loyal, college)

table; dining; dish, course

light

(lucid, translucent, illustrate, illuminate)

night

(nocturnal, equinox)

dessert

sómnus, sómnī (m)

quídam, quaédam, quíddam
(pron.)

quídam, quaédam, quóddam
(adj.)

pudícus, pudíca, pudícum

supérbus, supérba, supérbum

trístis, tríste

túrpis, túrpe

urbánus, urbána, urbánum

prae (+abl.)

quam
(adv. and conj.)

a certain one or thing, someone,
something

sleep

(somnambulate, insomnia)

modest, chaste

a certain, some

(impudent, pudency, pudendum)

sad, sorrowful;
joyless, grim, severe

arrogant, overbearing, haughty, proud

(triste, tristesse, tristful)

(superb, superbly)

of the city, urban;
urbane, elegant

ugly; shameful, base, disgraceful

(urbanization, suburban)

(turpitude)

than *(after comparatives)*
or
as . . . as possible *(with superlatives)*

in front of, before

(precede, prepare, preposition)

tántum

invítō, invītáre, invītávī, invītátum

dēlectátiō, dēlectātiónis (f)

népōs, nepótis (m)

sōl, sólis (m)

díligēns, *gen.* dīligéntis

dissímilis, dissímile

grácilis, grácile

húmilis, húmile

máior, máius

to entertain, invite, summon (invitation, vie)	only
grandson, descendant (nephew, nepotism, niece)	delight, pleasure, enjoyment (delectable, delicious)
diligent, careful (diligence, diligently)	sun (solar, solarium, solstice)
slender, thin (gracile, gracility)	unlike, different (dissimilar, dissemble)
greater; older (major, majority)	lowly, humble (humility, humiliate)

maiṓrēs, maiṓrum

prī́mus, prī́ma, prī́mum

quot

sī́milis, sī́mile (+gen. *or* dat.)

súperus, súpera, súperum

súperī, superṓrum (m. pl.)

ū́tilis, ū́tile

pṓnō, pṓnere, pósuī, pósitum

próbō, probā́re, probā́vī, probā́tum

bónus, mélior, óptimus

first, foremost, chief, principal

(primary, primate, prime, premier)

ancestors

similar (to), like, resembling

(similarly, simile, assimilate, simulate)

how many, as many as

(quota, quotation, quotient)

the gods

above, upper

(superior, superiority)

to put, place, set

(component, compound, deposit)

useful, advantageous

(utility, utilization)

good, better, best

(bona fide, ameliorate, optimist)

to approve, recommend; test

(probe, probation, proof, improve)

Chapter 27	(591)	Chapter 27	(592)

mágnus, máior, máximus

málus, péior, péssimus

Chapter 27	(593)	Chapter 27	(594)

múltus, plūs, plúrimus

párvus, mínor, mínimus

Chapter 27	(595)	Chapter 27	(596)

príor, prímus

súperus, supérior,
súmmus *or* suprémus

Chapter 28	(597)	Chapter 28	(598)

árma, armốrum (n. pl.)

cúrsus, cúrsūs (m)

Chapter 28	(599)	Chapter 28	(600)

lúna, lúnae (f)

occắsiō, occāsiốnis (f)

bad, worse, worst

(malaise, pejorative, pessimist)

great, greater, greatest

(magnify, majority, maximize)

small, smaller, smallest

(parvo virus, minority, minimize)

much, more, most

(multiply, plurality)

that above; higher;
highest, furthest *or* highest, last

(superiority, summit, supreme)

former, first

(prioritize, primacy)

running, race; course

(cursor, cursive, discourse)

arms, weapons

(armor, army, armada)

occasion, opportunity

(occasional, occasionalism)

moon

(lunar, lunacy, lunatic)

párēns, paréntis (m *or* f)   stélla, stéllae (f)

vésper, vésperis *or* vésperī (m)   mórtuus, mórtua, mórtuum

prínceps, príncipis (m *or* f)   prínceps, *gen.* príncipis

ut (+subjunctive)
or
ut (+indicative)   nē

cédō, cédere, céssī, céssum   dédicō, dēdicáre, dēdicávī, dēdicátum

star, planet

(stellar, constellation, interstellar)

parent

(parentage, parental)

dead

(mortician, mortuary)

evening; evening star

(vesper, vesperal, Vespers)

chief, foremost

(principal, principality)

leader, emperor

(prince, princely)

not; in order that . . . not, that . . . not,
in order not to

in order that, so that, that,
in order to, so as to, to
or
just as, as, when

to dedicate

(dedication, dedicatory)

to go, withdraw;
yield to, grant, submit

(accede, access, proceed, succeed)

égeō, egḗre, éguī (+abl. *or* gen.)

éxpleō, explḗre, explḗvī, explḗtum

praéstō, praestā́re, praéstitī, praéstitum

táceō, tacḗre, tácuī, tácitum

fā́tum, fā́tī (n)

ingénium, ingéniī (n)

moénia, moénium (n. pl.)

nā́ta, nā́tae (f)

ṓsculum, ṓsculī (n)

sī́dus, sī́deris (n)

to fill, fill up, complete

(expletive, deplete)

to need, lack, want

(indigence, indigent)

to be silent, leave unmentioned

(tacit, taciturn, reticent)

to excel; exhibit, show, offer, supply, furnish

nature, innate talent

(ingenuity, genius, genial)

fate; death

(fatal, fatality, fateful)

daughter

(prenatal, postnatal)

walls of a city

(munitions, ammunition)

constellation, star

(consider, desire, sidereal)

kiss

(osculate, osculation)

dígnus, dígna, dígnum (+abl.)

dū́rus, dū́ra, dū́rum

tántus, tánta, tántum

dénique

íta

(adv. used with adjs., vbs., and advs.)

quídem

nē . . . quídem

sīc

(adv. most commonly used with vbs.)

tam; tam...quam

tamquam

hard, harsh, rough, stern,
unfeeling, hardy, difficult

(dour, durable, during, endure)

worthy, worthy of

(dignify, indignation)

at last, finally, lastly

so large, so great, of such a size

(tantamount)

indeed, certainly, at least, even

so, thus

so, thus

not . . . even

(sic)

as it were, as if, so to speak

so, to such a degree; so...as

Chapter 29 (631)	Chapter 29 (632)
vḗrō	cóndō, cóndere, cóndidī, cónditum
Chapter 29 (633)	Chapter 29 (634)
conténdō, conténdere, conténdī, conténtum	mólliō, mollíre, mollívī, mollítum
Chapter 29 (635)	Chapter 29 (636)
púgnō, pugnáre, pugnávī, pugnátum	respóndeō, respondére, respóndī, respónsum
Chapter 29 (637)	Chapter 30 (638)
súrgō, súrgere, surréxī, surréctum	hónor, honóris (m)
Chapter 30 (639)	Chapter 30 (640)
céterī, céterae, cétera (pl.)	quántus, quánta, quántum

to put together *or* into, store;
found, establish

(condiment, abscond)

in truth, indeed, to be sure, however

(very, verily)

to soften; make calm *or* less hostile

(mollify, emollient)

to strive, struggle, contend; hasten

(contender, contentious)

to answer

(respond, responsibility, correspond)

to fight

(pugnacious, impugn, pugilist, pugilism)

honor, esteem; public office

(honorable, honorary, dishonor, honest)

to get up, arise

(surge, resurrection, source)

how large, how great, how much

(quantity, quantitative)

the remaining, the rest, the other,
all the others

(ceteris paribus, et cetera)

tántus . . . quántus

rīdículus, rīdícula, rīdículum

vívus, víva, vívum

fúrtim

mox

prímō

repénte

únde

útrum . . . an

bíbō, bíbere, bíbī

laughable, ridiculous

(deride, ridicule)

just as much (many) . . . as

stealthily, secretly

(furtively, ferret)

alive, living

(vivid, convivial)

at first, at the beginning

(primogenitor, primogeniture)

soon

whence, from what *or* which place,
from which, from whom

suddenly

to drink

(imbibe, beverage)

whether . . . or

Chapter 30 (651)	Chapter 30 (652)
cognōscō, cognōscere, cognōvī, cógnitum *or* nōscō, nōscere, nōvī, nōtum	comprehéndō, comprehéndere, comprehéndī, comprehḗnsum

Chapter 30 (653)	Chapter 30 (654)
cōnsū́mō, cōnsū́mere, cōnsū́mpsī, cōnsū́mptum	dúbitō, dubitáre, dubitávī, dubitátum

Chapter 30 (655)	Chapter 30 (656)
expṓnō, expṓnere, expósuī, expósitum	mínuō, minúere, mínuī, minū́tum

Chapter 30 (657)	Chapter 31 (658)
rógō, rogáre, rogávī, rogátum	as, ássis (m)

Chapter 31 (659)	Chapter 31 (660)
auxílium, auxíliī (n)	dígitus, dígitī (m)

to grasp, seize, arrest;
comprehend, understand

(comprehensive, comprehensible)

to become acquainted with, learn,
recognize; know *(in perfect tenses)*

(cognition, incognito, reconnoiter)

to doubt, hesitate

(dubious, doubtful, undoubtedly)

to consume, use up

(consumer, assume, presume, resume)

to lessen, diminish

(diminish, diminutive, minuet, menu)

to set forth, explain, expose

(exponent, exposition, expound)

an as *(a small copper coin)*

to ask

(interrogate, arrogant, prerogative)

finger, toe

(digit, digital, prestidigitation)

aid, help

(auxiliary)

elephántus, elephántī (m *or* f)

exsílium, exsíliī (n)

invídia, invídiae (f)

rűmor, rūmőris (m)

vínum, vínī (n)

medíocris, medíocre

cum (+subjunctive)
or
cum (+indicative)

ápud (+acc.)

sémel

úsque

exile, banishment

(exilian, exilic)

elephant

(elephantine, elephantiasis)

rumor, gossip

(rumormonger)

envy, jealousy, hatred

(invidious, envious)

ordinary, moderate, mediocre

(mediocritize, mediocrity)

wine

(vine, vinegar, vintage)

among, in the presence of,
at the house of

when, since, although
or
when

all the way, up (to), even (to),
continuously, always

a single time, once,
once and for all, simultaneously

dóleō, dolére, dólui, dolitúrum

dórmiō, dormíre, dormívī, dormítum

férō, férre, túlī, látum

ádferō, adférre, áttulī, allátum

cṓnferō, cōnférre, cóntulī, collátum

sē cōnférre

ófferō, offérre, óbtulī, oblátum

réferō, reférre, réttulī, relátum

invídeō, invidére, invídī, invísum

óccidō, occídere, óccidī, occásum

to sleep

(dormitory, dormer, dormant)

to grieve, suffer; hurt, give pain

(doleful, condole, indolent)

to bring to

(afferent)

to bear, carry, bring;
suffer, endure, tolerate; say, report

(circumference, fertile, confer, differ)

to go

to bring together, compare;
confer, bestow

(conference, collation)

to carry back, bring back;
repeat, answer, report

(refer, reference, relate, relative)

to offer

(oblation, offertory)

to fall down; die; set

(occidental, occasion)

to be envious;
or
to look at with envy, envy,
be jealous of (+dat.)

(invidious, invidiously)

custṓdia, custṓdiae (f)

exércitus, exércitūs (m)

paupértās, paupertátis (f)

díves, *gen.* dívitis *or* dítis

pār, *gen.* páris (+dat.)

paúper, *gen.* paúperis

dúmmodo (+subj.)

mā́lō, mā́lle, mā́luī

nṓlō, nṓlle, nṓluī

páteō, patḗre, pátuī

army

(exercise, exercitation)

protection, custody;
guards *(pl.)*

(custodian, custodial)

rich, wealthy

(Dives)

poverty, humble circumstances

of small means, poor

(impoverished, pauper, poverty)

equal, like

(pair, parity, peer, disparage)

to want (something) more, instead;
prefer

provided that, so long as

to be open, lie open,
be accessible; be evident

(patency, patent)

to not . . . wish, be unwilling

(nolens volens, nolo contendere, nolpros)

praébeō, praebére, praébuī, praébitum

prōmíttō, prōmíttere, prōmísī, prōmíssum

vólō, vélle, vóluī

lóngē, lóngius, longíssimē

líberē, lībérius, lībérrimē

púlchrē, púlchrius, pulchérrimē

fórtiter, fórtius, fortíssimē

celériter, celérius, celérrimē

ácriter, ácrius, ācérrimē

fēlíciter, fēlícius, fēlīcíssimē

to send forth; promise

(promissor, promissory)

to offer, provide

far, farther *or* too far,
farthest *or* very far

to wish, want, be willing, will

(volition, voluntary, benevolent)

beautifully, more beautifully,
most beautifully

(pulchritude, pulchritudinous)

freely, more freely,
most freely *or* very freely

(liberal, liberally)

quickly, more quickly, most quickly

(accelerate, celerity)

bravely, more bravely, most bravely

(fortify, fortitude)

happily, more happily, most happily

(felicitously, infelicitously)

keenly, more keenly, most keenly

(acridly, acrimoniously)

Chapter 32	(701)	Chapter 32	(702)
sapiénter, sapiéntius, sapientíssimē		fácile, facílius, facíllimē	

Chapter 32	(703)	Chapter 32	(704)
béne, mélius, óptimē		mále, peíus, péssimē	

Chapter 32	(705)	Chapter 32	(706)
múltum, plūs, plŭrimum		magnópere, mágis, máxime	

Chapter 32	(707)	Chapter 32	(708)
párum, mínus, mínimē		príus, prímō *or* prímum	

Chapter 32	(709)	Chapter 33	(710)
díū, diútius, diūtíssimē		inítium, inítiī (n)	

easily, more easily, most easily

(facile, facilely)

wisely, more wisely, most wisely

(sapiently, insipidly)

badly, worse, worst

(maliciously, pejoratively, pessimistically)

well, better, best

(beneficially, ameliorate, optimally)

greatly; more *(quality)*;
most, especially

(magnificently, magisterially, maximally)

much; more *(quantity)*;
most, very much

(multilaterally, plurally)

before, earlier; first *(in time)*, at first, *or*
first *(in a series)*, in the first place

(priority, primarily)

little, not very (much); less; least

(minority, minimally)

beginning, commencement

(initial, initiation)

for a long time, longer, very long

ops, ópis (f)

ópēs, ópum (f. pl.)

philósophus, philósophī (m)
and
philósopha, philósophae (f)

plēbs, plébis (f)

sāl, sális (m)

spéculum, spéculī (n)

quis, quid (*after* sī, nisi, nē, num)

cándidus, cándida, cándidum

mérus, méra, mérum

suávis, suáve

power, resources, wealth

(opulent, opulence)

help, aid

the common people,
populace, plebeians

(plebs, plebeian)

philosopher

(philosophy, philosophical)

mirror

(speculate, speculation)

salt; wit

(salad, saline, salary)

shining, bright, white; beautiful

(candid, candidate, incandescent)

anyone, anything, someone,
something

sweet

(suave, dissuade, persuasion)

pure, undiluted

(mere, merely)

-ve

heu

súbitō

recū́sō, recūsā́re, recūsā́vī, recūsā́tum

trā́dō, trā́dere, trā́didī, trā́ditum

ánima, ánimae (f)

remíssiō, remissiốnis (f)

vōx, vốcis (f)

advérsus, advérsa, advérsum

tā́lis, tā́le

ah! alas!

or

to refuse

suddenly

(recuse, recusant)

(sudden, suddenness)

air *(breathed by an animal),* breath;
soul, spirit

to give over, surrender;
hand down, transmit, teach

(animation, inanimate)

(tradition, traitor, treason)

voice, word

letting go, release; relaxation

(vocal, vocalize, vowel)

(remiss, remission)

such, of such a sort

opposite, adverse

(adversary, adversely, adversity)

vae (often +dat. or acc.)

árbitror, arbitrắrī, arbitrắtus sum

cốnor, cōnắrī, cōnắtus sum

crếscō, crếscere, crếvī, crếtum

ēgrédior, égredī, ēgréssus sum

fáteor, fatḗrī, fássus sum

hórtor, hortắrī, hortắtus sum

lóquor, lóquī, locútus sum

mốlior, mōlĩrī, mōlītus sum

mórior, mórī, mórtuus sum,
moritúrus *(fut. act. part.)*

to judge, think

(arbiter, arbitration, arbitrary)

alas, woe to

to increase

(crescendo, decrease, increment, accrue)

to try, attempt

(conation, conative)

to confess, admit

(confess, confession, profess)

to go out

(congress, degrade, digress, egress)

to say, speak, tell

(loquacious, colloquial, elocution)

to encourage, urge

(hortatory, exhort, exhortation)

to die

(moribund, mortuary)

to work at, build, undertake, plan

(demolish, demolition)

Chapter 34 (741)	Chapter 34 (742)
náscor, náscī, nátus sum	pátior, pátī, pássus sum
Chapter 34 (743)	Chapter 34 (744)
proficíscor, proficíscī, proféctus sum	rústicor, rūsticárī, rūsticátus sum
Chapter 34 (745)	Chapter 34 (746)
sédeō, sedére, sḗdī, séssum	séquor, séquī, secútus sum
Chapter 34 (747)	Chapter 34 (748)
spéctō, spectáre, spectávī, spectátum	útor, útī, úsus sum (+abl.)
Chapter 35 (749)	Chapter 35 (750)
aéstās, aestátis (f)	iánua, iánuae (f)

to suffer, endure; permit

(passion, passive, patient)

to be born; spring forth, arrive

(cognate, innate, natal, nation)

to live in the country

(rustic, rusticate, rural)

to set out, start

to follow

(consequent, sequence, sequel)

to sit

(sedan, sedate, sediment, siege, president)

to use; enjoy, experience

(abuse, peruse, usual, utensil, utilize)

to look at, see

(spectator, aspect, respect, suspect)

door

(janitor, January)

summer

(estival, estivation)

péctus, péctoris (n)

praémium, praémiī (n)

īrắtus, īrắta, īrắtum

antepṓnō, antepṓnere, antepósuī, antepósitum

fóveō, fovḗre, fṓvī, fṓtum

ignṓscō, ignṓscere, ignṓvī, ignṓtum (+dat.)

ímperō, imperắre, imperắvī, imperắtum (+dat.)

míror, mīrắrī, mīrắtus sum

nóceō, nocḗre, nócuī, nócitum (+dat.)

nū́bō, nū́bere, nū́psī, nū́ptum

reward, prize

(premium)

breast, heart

(pectoral, expectorate, parapet)

to put before, prefer

angry

(irascible, irate)

to grant pardon to, forgive

to comfort, nurture, cherish

(foment)

to marvel at, admire, wonder

(admire, marvel, mirage, mirror)

to give orders to, command

(imperative, emperor)

to cover, veil
or
to be married to, marry (+dat.)

(nubile, nuptials)

to do harm to, harm, injure

(innocent, innocuous, obnoxious)

Chapter 35   (761)

párcō, párcere, pepércī, parsúrum
(+dat.)

Chapter 35   (762)

páreō, pārére, páruī (+dat.)

Chapter 35   (763)

persuádeō, persuādére, persuásī,
persuásum (+dat.)

Chapter 35   (764)

pláceō, placére, plácuī, plácitum
(+dat.)

Chapter 35   (765)

sápiō, sápere, sapívī

Chapter 35   (766)

sérviō, servíre, servívī, servítum
(+dat.)

Chapter 35   (767)

stúdeō, studére, stúduī (+dat.)

Chapter 35   (768)

subrídeō, subrīdére, subrísī, subrísum

Chapter 36   (769)

cupídō, cupídinis (f)

Chapter 36   (770)

léctor, lēctóris (m)
and
léctrīx, lēctrícis (f)

to be obedient to, obey

(apparent, appear)

to be lenient to, spare

(parsimonious, parsimony)

to be pleasing to, please

(complacent, implacable, placid, pleasure)

to succeed in urging, persuade, convince

(assuage, dissuade, suave)

to be a slave to, serve

(service, subservient, deserve)

to have good taste; have good sense, be wise

(sapient, insipid, sage, savor)

to smile (down) upon

(deride, risible)

to direct one's zeal to, be eager for, study

(student, studious)

reader

(lectern, lector)

desire, compassion

(Cupid, cupidity)

vínculum, vínculī (n)

cōtídiē

fortásse

accédō, accédere, accéssī, accéssum

cárpō, cárpere, cárpsī, cárptum

cốgō, cốgere, coḗgī, coáctum

contémnō, contémnere, contémpsī,
contémptum

contúndō, contúndere, cóntudī,
contúsum

cū́rō, cūrā́re, cūrā́vī, cūrátum

dēcérnō, dēcérnere, dēcrḗvī, dēcrétum

daily, every day

(quotidian)

bond, chain, fetter

(vinculum)

to come (to), approach

(accede, access, accessory)

perhaps

to drive *or* bring together,
force, compel

(cogent, coagulate)

to harvest, pluck; seize

(excerpt, carpet, scarce)

to beat, crush, bruise, destroy

(contuse, contusion)

to despise, scorn

(contempt, contemptuous)

to decide, settle, decree

(decretal, decretory)

to care for, attend to; heal, cure;
take care

(cure, curator, procure, accurate)

éxigō, exígere, exḗgī, exáctum

fíō, fíerī, fáctus sum

obléctō, oblectáre, oblectávī, oblectátum

ŕrō, ōrĽre, ōrávī, ōrátum

récreō, recreáre, recreávī, recreátum

requírō, requírere, requīsívī, requīsítum

serénō, serēnáre, serēnávī, serēnátum

Athénae, Athēnárum (f. pl.)

dómus, dómūs *or* dómī (f)

dómī

to occur, happen; become;
be made, be done

(fact, fiat)

to drive out, force out, exact;
drive through, complete, perfect

(exactitude, exigent)

to speak, plead;
beg, beseech, entreat, pray

(orator, oration, oracle, adore)

to please, amuse, delight;
pass time pleasantly

(delectable, delectation)

to seek, ask for; miss, need, require

(requirement, requisite, request)

to restore, revive; refresh, cheer

(recreate, recreation)

Athens

to make clear, brighten;
cheer up, soothe

(serene, serenity, serenade)

at home

house, home

(domain, domicile, domestic)

dómum

dómō

húmus, húmī (f)

íter, itíneris (n)

rūs, rū́ris (n)

Syrācū́sae, Syrācūsā́rum (f. pl.)

ábsēns, *gen.* abséntis

grā́tus, grā́ta, grā́tum

idṓneus, idṓnea, idṓneum

immṓtus, immṓta, immṓtum

from home	(to) home
journey; route, road	ground, earth; soil
(itinerant, itinerary)	(exhume, posthumous)
Syracuse	the country, countryside
	(rustic, rusticity)
pleasing, agreeable; grateful	absent, away
(grace, gracious, gratuity, agree)	(absence, absentee)
unmoved; unchanged; unrelenting	suitable, fit, appropriate
(immotile)	

fórīs

éō, íre, íī, ítum

ábeō, abíre, ábiī, ábitum

ádeō, adíre, ádiī, áditum

éxeō, exíre, éxiī, éxitum

íneō, iníre, íniī, ínitum

óbeō, obíre, óbiī, óbitum

péreō, períre, périī, péritum

rédeō, redíre, rédiī, réditum

interfíciō, interfícere, interfḗcī,
interféctum

to go

(ambition, circuit, sedition, transit)

out of doors, outside

(foreclose, foreign, forest, forfeit)

to go to, approach

(adit)

to go away, depart, leave

to enter into, begin

(initiate, initiative)

to go out, exit

to pass away, be destroyed, perish

to go up against, meet; die

(obiter dictum, obituary)

to kill, murder

to go back, return

lícet, licḗre, lícuit (+dat. +infin.)

peregrī́nor, peregrīnā́rī,
peregrīnā́tus sum

requiḗscō, requiḗscere, requiḗvī,
requiḗtum

sóleō, solḗre, sólitus sum

árbor, árboris (f)

dígnitās, dignitā́tis (f)

dólor, dolṓris (m)

ódium, ódiī (n)

ópus, óperis (n)

ōrā́tiō, ōrātiṓnis (f)

to travel abroad, wander

(peregrine, pilgrim, pilgrimage)

it is permitted *(for someone to do something),* one may

(license, illicit, leisure)

to be accustomed

(insolent, obsolete)

to rest

(requiescat, requiem)

merit, prestige, dignity

(dignify, indignity)

tree

(arbor, arboreal, arboriculture)

hatred

(odious, annoy)

pain, grief

(doleful, condolences, indolent)

speech

(oration, oratorical)

a work, task; deed, accomplishment

(opera, operate, cooperate)

pēs, pédis (m)

sátor, satóris (m)

fírmus, fírma, fírmum

īnfírmus, īnfírma, īnfírmum

mīrábilis, mīrábile

prístinus, prístina, prístinum

sublímis, sublíme

étsī

érga (+acc.)

libénter

sower, planter;
begetter, father; founder

lower leg, foot

(pedal, pedestal, pedestrian, impede)

not strong, weak, feeble

firm, strong; reliable

(infirm, infirmary, infirmity)

(firmament, affirm, confirm)

ancient; former, previous

amazing, wondrous, remarkable

(pristine, pristinely)

(admirable, marvel)

even if, although

elevated, lofty; heroic, noble

(sublime, sublimate)

with pleasure, gladly

toward

impédiō, impedī́re, impedī́vī,
impedī́tum

métuō, metúere, métuī

quéror, quérī, quéstus sum

recognṓscō, recognṓscere, recognṓvī,
recógnitum

suspéndō, suspéndere, suspéndī,
suspénsum

vḗndō, vḗndere, vḗndidī, vḗnditum

aedifícium, aedifíciī (n)

iniū́ria, iniū́riae (f)

múlier, mulíeris (f)

trā́nsitus, trā́nsitūs (m)

to fear, dread, be afraid for (+dat.)

(meticulous, meticulousness)

to impede, hinder, prevent

(impediment, impeach)

to recognize, recollect

(recognition, reconnaissance)

to complain, lament

(quarrel, querulous)

to sell

(vend, vendor)

to hang up, suspend; interrupt

(suspense, suspension)

injustice, injury, wrong

(injurious, injuriousness)

building, structure

(edification, edifice, edify)

passing over, transit; transition

(transitional, transitory)

woman

(muliebrity)

véntus, véntī (m)

cúpidus, cúpida, cúpidum

līberális, līberále

necésse

vétus, *gen.* véteris

quási

ámbulō, ambuláre, ambulávī, ambulátum

expérior, experírī, expértus sum

líbō, lībáre, lībávī, lībátum

opórtet, oportére, opórtuit (+infin.)

desirous, eager, fond;

or

desirous of, eager for (+gen.)

(cupidity)

wind

(vent, ventilation)

necessary, inevitable

(necessitate, unnecessary)

of, relating to a free person;

worthy of a free man, decent, liberal;

generous

(liberalism, liberality)

as if, as it were

(quasi; *prefix* quasi-, quasi-official)

old

(veteran, veterinarian)

to try, test; experience

(experiment, expert, inexperience)

to walk

(amble, ambulance, perambulate)

it is proper, right, necessary

to pour a libation of, on; pour ritually;

sip; touch gently

(libation)

Chapter 39 (851)	Chapter 39 (852)
oppúgnō, oppugnā́re, oppugnā́vī, oppugnā́tum	ṓrnō, ōrnā́re, ōrnā́vī, ornā́tum

Chapter 39 (853)	Chapter 39 (854)
pernóctō, pernoctā́re, pernoctā́vī, pernoctā́tum	trā́nseō, trānsī́re, trā́nsiī, trā́nsitum

Chapter 40 (855)	Chapter 40 (856)
aes, aéris (n)	dóminus, dóminī (m)

Chapter 40 (857)	Chapter 40 (858)
dómina, dóminae (f)	lácrima, lácrimae (f)

Chapter 40 (859)	Chapter 40 (860)
mḗta, mḗtae (f)	monuméntum, monuméntī (n)

to equip, furnish, adorn

(adornment, ornate, ornamental)

to fight against, attack,
assault, assail

(oppugn, oppugner)

to go across, cross;
pass over, ignore

(transit, transition, transitory)

to spend *or* occupy the night

(nocturnal, nocturne)

master (of a household), lord

(dominate, domain, dungeon)

bronze

(era)

tear

(lacrimal, lacrimation)

mistress, lady

(dame, damsel, madonna)

monument

(monumental, monumentalize)

turning point, goal; limit, boundary

nắsus, nắsī (m)

sáxum, sáxī (n)

vúltus, vúltūs (m)

iứstus, iứsta, iứstum

tot / tot...quot

praéter (+acc.)

nốnne

num

omnī́nō

postrḗmum

rock, stone

(saxatile, saxifrage)

nose

(nasal, nasalize)

just, right

(justice, unjust, justification, adjust)

countenance, face

besides, except; beyond, past

(preterit, preterition, preternatural)

so many, as many / as many...as

(total, totality)

1. introduces direct questions
which expect the answer "no"

2. introduces indirect question
and means *whether*

introduces questions expecting
the answer "yes"

after all, finally;
for the last time

(postnatal, post-war)

wholly, entirely, altogether;
(with negatives) at all

(omnipotent, omniscient)

quīn

éxplicō, explicáre, explicávī, explicátum

fatígō, fatīgáre, fatīgávī, fatīgátum

for, fárī, fátus sum

opínor, opīnárī, opīnátus sum

repériō, reperíre, répperī, repértum

véreor, verérī, véritus sum

to unfold; explain;
spread out, deploy

(explicate, inexplicable)

indeed, in fact, furthermore

to speak (prophetically),
talk, foretell

(affable, fate, infant, infantry)

to weary, tire out

(fatigue, indefatigable)

to find, discover, learn; get

(repertoire, repertory)

to suppose

(opine, opinion)

to show reverence for, respect;
be afraid of, fear

(revere, reverend, irreverent)

Alphabetical Listing of Vocabulary For Wheelock's Latin, Chapters 1-40

Each vocabulary entry is followed by its card number. Cardinal numerals and ordinal numerals appear at the end of this list.

ā (ab)	300	animus	96	cadō	265	cōnsul	234	dēnique	624
abeō	803	annus	252	caecus	379	cōnsūmō	653	dēsīderō	389
absēns	797	ante	277	caelum	98	contemnō	777	deus	121
accēdō	774	antepōnō	754	Caesar	254	contendō	633	dexter	443
accipiō	527	antīquus	40	candidus	718	contineō	467	dīcō	227
ācer	362	appellō	302	capiō	226	contrā	425	diēs	474
acerbus	260	apud	668	caput	233	contundō	778	difficilis	365
ācriter	699	aqua	285	careō	445	cōpia	167	digitus	660
ad	177	arbitror	732	carmen	143	cōpiae	168	dignitās	816
adeō	804	arbor	815	carpō	775	cornū	431	dignus	621
adferō	674	argūmentum	410	Carthāgō	516	corpus	145	dīligēns	576
adiuvō	93	arma	597	cārus	241	cōtīdiē	772	dīligō	281
admittō	385	ars	286	casa	451	crās	110	discēdō	447
adulēscēns	251	arx	494	causa	452	crēdō	544	discipula	135
adulēscentia	95	as	658	causā	453	creō	266	discipulus	122
adversus	729	Asia	253	cēdō	609	crēscō	734	discō	184
aedificium	837	asper	464	celer	364	culpa	99	dissimilis	577
aequus	482	at	423	celeriter	698	culpō	117	diū	262
aes	855	Athēnae	788	cēna	553	cum *(prep.)*	224	diū *(comp.)*	709
aestās	749	atque (ac)	465	cēnō	116	cum *(conj.)*	667	dīves	684
aetās	357	auctor	411	cernō	490	cupiditās	214	dīvitiae	267
ager	51	audeō	164	certus	420	cupīdō	769	dō	11
agō	181	audiō	225	cēterī	639	cupidus	842	doceō	185
agricola	52	audītor	358	Cicerō	166	cupiō	387	doctus	273
āit	543	auris	287	cito	383	cūr	403	doleō	671
aliī...aliī	200	aut	381	cīvis	288	cūra	74	dolor	817
aliquis	503	aut...aut	382	cīvitās	144	cūrō	779	domī	790
alius	199	autem	245	clārus	401	currō	303	domina	857
alō	280	auxilium	659	clēmentia	359	cursus	598	dominus	856
alter	201	avārus	62	coepī	386	custōdia	681	domō	792
amābō tē	8	āvertō	514	cōgitō	9	dē	65	domum	791
ambulō	847	bāsium	71	cognōscō/nōscō	651	dea	120	domus	789
amīca	53	beātus	222	cōgō	776	dēbeō	10	dōnum	75
amīcitia	213	bellum	72	committō	316	dēcernō	780	dormiō	672
amīcus *(n.)*	53	bellus	85	commūnis	442	dēdicō	610	dubitō	654
amīcus *(adj.)*	240	bene	246	comprehendō	652	dēfendō	446	dūcō	186
āmittō	264	bene *(cp.)*	703	condō	632	dehinc	541	dulcis	366
amō	7	beneficium	412	cōnferō	675	deinde	404	dum	176
amor	142	bibō	650	coniūrātī	430	dēlectātiō	573	dummodo	687
anima	726	bonus	86	cōnor	733	dēlectō	427	dūrus	622
animal	284	bonus *(cp.)*	590	cōnservō	18	dēleō	388	dux	495
animī	97	brevis	363	cōnsilium	73	dēmōnstrō	183	ēducō	507

Word	№	Word	№	Word	№	Word	№	Word	№
egeō	611	fidēlis	537	homō	146	invītō	572	loca	192
ego	236	fidēs	476	honor	638	ipse	270	locī	193
ēgredior	735	fīlia	55	hōra	215	īra	27	locus	191
elephantus	661	fīlius	56	hortor	737	īrātus	753	longē	694
enim	210	fīnēs	456	hostēs	397	is	238	longus	371
eō	802	fīnis	455	hostis	396	iste	198	loquor	738
equus	496	fīō	782	hūmānus	87	ita	625	lūdus	398
ergā	829	fīrmus	823	humilis	579	Italia	307	lūna	599
ēripiō	491	flūmen	394	humus	793	itaque	315	lūx	557
errō	12	fluō	405	iaceō	545	iter	794	magister	77
est	50	for	874	iaciō	318	iterum	466	magistra	77
et	45	forīs	801	iam	426	iubeō	468	magnanimus	505
et...et	46	fōrma	25	iānua	750	iūcundus	370	magnopere	706
etiam	247	fortasse	773	ibi	137	iūdex	415	magnus	41
etsī	828	fortis	368	īdem	239	iūdicium	416	magnus (cp.)	591
ex (ē)	178	fortiter	697	idōneus	799	iungō	282	maior	580
excipiō	528	fortūna	26	igitur	107	iūs	289	maiōrēs	581
exeō	805	fortūnātus	274	ignis	477	iūstus	864	male	704
exercitus	682	forum	554	ignōscō	756	iuvō	93	mālō	688
exigō	781	foveō	755	ille	197	labor	147	malus	88
exitium	76	frāter	169	immortālis	422	labōrō	469	malus (cp.)	592
expellō	531	frūctus	432	immōtus	800	lacrima	858	maneō	118
experior	848	fugiō	229	impediō	831	Latīnus	485	manus	434
expleō	612	fūrtim	644	imperātor	518	laudō	13	mare	290
explicō	872	gaudeō	508	imperium	519	laus	170	māter	255
expōnō	655	geminus	538	imperō	757	lēctor	770	mē	1
exsilium	662	gēns	457	in (+abl.)	66	lēctrīx	770	medica	256
exspectō	317	genū	433	in (+acc.)	211	legō	406	medicus	256
fābula	517	genus	395	incertus	484	levis	380	mediocris	666
facile	702	gerō	187	incipiō	390	lēx	555	medius	486
facilis	367	glōria	100	ineō	806	libellus	377	memoria	308
faciō	228	gracilis	578	īnfirmus	824	libenter	830	mēns	360
factum	268	Graecia	414	ingenium	616	līber	103	mēnsa	558
fāma	24	Graecus (adj.)	127	ingēns	369	liber	124	mēnsa secunda	559
familia	413	Graecus (n.)	128	initium	710	līberālis	843	merus	719
fateor	736	grātiās agere	182	iniūria	838	līberē	695	mēta	859
fatīgō	873	grātus	798	inquit	492	līberō	428	metuō	832
fātum	615	gravis	421	īnsidiae	123	lībertās	171	metus	435
fēlīciter	700	habeō	69	īnsula	498	lībō	849	meus	42
fēlīx	483	hasta	497	intellegō	248	licet	811	mīles	500
fēmina	54	heri	111	inter	314	līmen	556	minuō	656
fenestra	454	heu	722	interficiō	810	lingua	535	mīrābilis	825
ferō	673	hic	196	inveniō	231	littera	148	mīror	758
ferōx	536	hīc	542	invideō	679	litterae	149	misceō	407
ferrum	475	hodiē	67	invidia	663	lītus	499	miser	313

mittō	249	neque...neque	244	ōrātiō	820	plēnus	130	quandō	112
modus	478	nesciō	547	ōrātor	501	poena	32	quantus	640
moenia	617	neuter	202	ōrnō	852	poenās dare	33	quārē	139
mōlior	739	nihil	3 & 79	ōrō	784	poēta	34	quasi	846
molliō	634	nimis	212	ōs	293	pōnō	588	-que	134
moneō	14	nimium	212	ōsculum	619	populus	58	queror	833
mōns	436	nisi	424	ostendō	509	porta	35	quī *(pron.)*	378
monumentum	860	noceō	759	ōtium	82	possum	140	quī *(adj.)*	419
mora	78	nōlō	689	pār	685	post	162	quid	2
morbus	194	nōmen	152	parcō	761	posteā	526	quīdam *(adj.)*	563
mōrēs	151	nōn	4	parēns	601	postrēmum	870	quīdam *(pron.)*	562
morior	740	nōn sōlum...	205	pāreō	762	potēns	373	quidem	626
mors	291	nōnne	867	parō	429	prae	569	quīn	871
mortālis	402	noster	104	pars	294	praebeō	691	quis *(indef.)*	717
mortuus	604	novus	161	parum	707	praemium	752	quis *(int.)*	418
mōs	150	nox	560	parvus	89	praestō	613	quisque	271
moveō	408	nūbēs	292	parvus *(cp.)*	594	praeter	866	quisquis	504
mox	645	nūbō	760	patefaciō	549	premō	511	quod	242
mulier	839	nūllus	203	pateō	690	prīmō	646	quondam	487
multum	705	num	868	pater	257	prīmus	345 & 582	quoniam	223
multus	43	numerus	57	patientia	258	prīnceps *(adj.)*	606	quoque	384
multus *(cp.)*	593	numquam	179	patior	742	prīnceps *(n.)*	605	quot	583
mundus	458	nunc	138	patria	29	prīncipium	259	rapiō	470
mūtō	304	nūntiō	548	paucī	63	prior	595	ratiō	172
nam	276	nūper	263	pauper	686	prīstinus	826	re- (red-)	524
nārrō	532	ō	48	paupertās	683	prius	708	recipiō	529
nāscor	741	obeō	807	pāx	153	prō	261	recitō	393
nāsus	861	oblectō	783	pectus	751	probitās	399	recognōscō	834
nāta	618	occāsiō	600	pecūnia	30	probō	589	recreō	785
nātūra	216	occidō	680	pellō	530	proficīscor	743	recūsō	724
nauta	28	oculus	80	per	278	prohibeō	449	redeō	809
nāvigō	391	ōdī	448	peregrīnor	812	prōmittō	692	referō	678
nāvis	459	odium	818	pereō	808	prōnūntiō	450	rēgīna	154
nē	608	offerō	677	perfugium	520	propter	109	regō	376
-ne	108	officium	81	perīculum	83	prōtinus	489	relinquō	471
nē...quidem	627	ōlim	279	pernoctō	853	pudīcus	564	remaneō	118
nec	243	omnīnō	869	perpetuus	129	puella	36	remedium	84
nec...nec	244	omnis	372	persuādeō	763	puer	59	remissiō	727
necesse	844	opēs	712	pēs	821	pugnō	635	repente	647
necō	165	opīnor	875	petō	510	pulcher	105	reperiō	876
neglegō	392	oportet	850	philosopha	713	pulchrē	696	requiēscō	813
negō	546	opprimō	512	philosophia	31	putō	550	requīrō	786
nēmō	235	oppugnō	851	philosophus	713	quaerō	533	rēs	479
nepōs	574	ops	711	placeō	764	quam *(adv.)*	375	rēs pūblica	480
neque	243	opus	819	plēbs	714	quam *(conj.)*	570	respondeō	636

revertō	515	sequor	746	suscipiō	552	ūnus	208	vīvō	232
rēx	155	serēnō	787	suspendō	835	urbānus	568	vīvus	643
rīdeō	534	serva	521	suus	275	urbs	297	vocō	23
rīdiculus	642	serviō	766	Syrācūsae	796	usque	670	volō	693
rogō	657	servitūs	439	taceō	614	ut *(+indic.)*	525	voluptās	221
Rōma	295	servō	17	tālis	730	ut *(+subjunct.)*	607	vōx	728
Rōmānus	64	servus	521	tam	629	uter	209	vulgus	463
rosa	37	sī	6	tam...quam	629	ūtilis	587	vulnus	523
rūmor	664	sī quandō	113	tamquam	630	ūtor	748	vultus	863
rūs	795	sīc	628	tamen	180	utrum...an	649		
rūsticor	744	sīdus	620	tangō	473	uxor	158	**Cardinal Numerals**	
sacerdōs	502	signum	269	tantum	571	vae	731	I – XXV	320 – 344
saepe	5	similis	584	tantus	623	valē	21	centum	310
sāl	715	sine	49	tantus..quantus	641	valeō	20	mīlia	312
salūs	460	sinister	444	tē	102	-ve	721	mīlle	311
salvē	16	sōl	575	tempestās	309	vēndō	836		
salveō	15	sōlācium	522	tempus	156	veniō	230	**Ordinal Numerals**	
salvus	131	soleō	814	teneō	305	ventus	841	prīmus - duodecimus	
sānus	106	sōlus	204	terra	157	verbum	101	345-356	
sapiēns	539	somnus	561	terreō	19	vereor	877		
sapienter	701	soror	174	timeō	319	vēritās	219	**Abbreviations**	
sapientia	60	spectō	747	timor	218	vērō	631	abl.	ablative
sapiō	765	speculum	716	tolerō	141	versus	441	acc.	accusative
satiō	70	spērō	551	tollō	493	vertō	513	adj.	adjective
satis	114	spēs	481	tot/tot...quot	865	vērus	92	adv.	adverb
sator	822	spīritus	440	tōtus	206	vesper	603	conj.	conjunction
satura	361	stēlla	602	trādō	725	vester	133	cp.	comparison
saxum	862	stō	283	trahō	189	vetus	845	indef.	indefinite
scelus	417	studeō	767	trāns	301	via	220	indic.	indicative
scientia	400	studium	195	trānseō	854	vīcīna	462	inter.	interrogative
sciō	472	stultus *(adj.)*	90	trānsitus	840	vīcīnus	462	n.	noun
scrībō	188	stultus *(n.)*	91	trīstis	565	victōria	175	prep.	preposition
scrīptor	173	suāvis	720	Trōia	461	videō	22	subjunct.	subjunctive
sē cōnferre	676	sub	163	tū	237	videor	409		
secundus	132	subitō	723	tum	115	vincō	190		
sed	47	sublīmis	827	turba	296	vinculum	771		
sedeō	745	subrīdeō	768	turpis	567	vīnum	665		
semel	669	suī	272	tuus	44	vir	61		
semper	68	sum	94	tyrannus	125	vīrēs	299		
senātus	437	superbus	565	ubi	136	virgō	159		
senectūs	217	superī	586	ūllus	207	virtūs	160		
senex	374	superō	119	ultimus	540	vīs	298		
sēnsus	438	superus	585	ultrā	488	vīta	39		
sententia	38	superus *(cp.)*	596	umquam	506	vitium	126		
sentiō	250	surgō	637	unde	648	vītō	306		

SUMMARY OF FORMS
FOR WHEELOCK'S LATIN

NOUNS—DECLENSIONS

First	Second				Third	
porta, -ae	amīcus, -ī	puer, -ī	ager, -grī	dōnum, -ī	rēx, rēgis	corpus, -oris
f., *gate*	m., *friend*	m., *boy*	m., *field*	n., *gift*	m., *king*	n., *body*
Sg.						
N. port-a	amīc-us[1]	puer	ager	dōn-um	rēx	corpus
G. port-ae	amīc-ī	puer-ī	agr-ī	dōn-ī	rēg-is	corpor-is
D. port-ae	amīc-ō	puer-ō	agr-ō	dōn-ō	rēg-ī	corpor-ī
A. port-am	amīc-um	puer-um	agr-um	dōn-um	rēg-em	corpus
Ab. port-ā	amīc-ō	puer-ō	agr-ō	dōn-ō	rēg-e	corpor-e
Pl.						
N. port-ae	amīc-ī	puer-ī	agr-ī	dōn-a	rēg-ēs	corpor-a
G. port-ārum	amīc-ōrum	puer-ōrum	agr-ōrum	dōn-ōrum	rēg-um	corpor-um
D. port-īs	amīc-īs	puer-īs	agr-īs	dōn-īs	rēg-ibus	corpor-ibus
A. port-ās	amīc-ōs	puer-ōs	agr-ōs	dōn-a	rēg-ēs	corpor-a
Ab. port-īs	amīc-īs	puer-īs	agr-īs	dōn-īs	rēg-ibus	corpor-ibus

Third (I-Stems)			Fourth		Fifth
cīvis, -is	urbs, -is	mare, -is	frūctus, -ūs	cornū,-ūs	diēs, -ēī
m., *citizen*	f., *city*	n., *sea*	m., *fruit*	n., *horn*	m., *day*
Sg.					
N. cīv-is	urb-s	mar-e	frūct-us	corn-ū	di-ēs
G. cīv-is	urb-is	mar-is	frūct-ūs	corn-ūs	di-ēī
D. cīv-ī	urb-ī	mar-ī	frūct-uī	corn-ū	di-ēī
A. cīv-em	urb-em	mar-e	frūct-um	corn-ū	di-em
Ab. cīv-e	urb-e	mar-ī	frūct-ū	corn-ū	di-ē
Pl.					
N. cīv-ēs	urb-ēs	mar-ia	frūct-ūs	corn-ua	di-ēs
G. cīv-ium	urb-ium	mar-ium	frūct-uum	corn-uum	di-ērum
D. cīv-ibus	urb-ibus	mar-ibus	frūct-ibus	corn-ibus	di-ēbus
A. cīv-ēs	urb-ēs	mar-ia	frūct-ūs	corn-ua	di-ēs
Ab. cīv-ibus	urb-ibus	mar-ibus	frūct-ibus	corn-ibus	di-ēbus

Vīs is irregular: Sg., N., vīs, G. (vīs), D. (vī), A. vim. Ab. vī; Pl., N. vīrēs, G. vīrium, D. vīribus, A. vīrēs, Ab. vīribus.

[1] The vocative singular of nouns like **amīcus** and of masculine adjectives like **magnus** ends in **-e**. The vocative singular of **fīlius** and of names in **-ius** ends in a single **-ī** (**fīlī, Vergilī**); the vocative singular of the masculine adjective **meus** is **mī**; the vocative singular of masculine adjectives in **-ius** ends in **-ie** (**ēgregius; ēgregie**). Otherwise, the vocative has the same form as the nominative in all declensions.

ADJECTIVES—DECLENSIONS

First and Second Declensions

	Adjs. in -us, -a, -um			Adjs. in -er, -era, -erum; -er, -ra, -rum		
M.	**F.**	**N.**		**M.**	**F.**	**N.**
	Singular				**Singular²**	
N. magnus	magna	magnum		līber	lībera	līberum
G. magnī	magnae	magnī		līberī	līberae	līberī
D. magnō	magnae	magnō		līberō	līberae	līberō
A. magnum	magnam	magnum		līberum	līberam	līberum
Ab. magnō	magnā	magnō		līberō	līberā	līberō
	Plural				**Singular²**	
N. magnī	magnae	magna		pulcher	pulchra	pulchrum
G. magnōrum	magnārum	magnōrum		pulchrī	pulchrae	pulchrī
D. magnīs	magnīs	magnīs		pulchrō	pulchrae	pulchrō
A. magnōs	magnās	magna		pulchrum	pulchram	pulchrum
Ab. magnīs	magnīs	magnīs		pulchrō	pulchrā	pulchrō

Third Declension

Two endings		**Three endings**		**One Ending**		**Comparatives⁵**	
fortis, forte		ācer, ācris, ācre		potēns³		fortior, fortius	
brave		*keen, severe*		*powerful*		*braver*	
M. & F.	**N.**	**M. & F.**	**N.**	**M. & F.**	**N.**	**M. & F.**	**N.**
Sg.							
N. fortis	forte	ācer ācris	ācre	potēns	potēns	fortior	fortius
G. fortis		ācris		potentis		fortiōris	
D. fortī		ācrī		potentī		fortiōrī	
A. fortem	forte	ācrem	ācre	potentem	potēns	fortiōrem	fortius
Ab. fortī		ācrī		potentī		fortiōre	
Pl.							
N. fortēs	fortia	ācrēs	ācria	potentēs	potentia	fortiōrēs	fortiōra
G. fortium		ācrium		potentium		fortiōrum	
D. fortibus		ācribus		potentibus		fortiōribus	
A. fortēs⁴	fortia	ācres⁴	ācria	potentēs⁴	potentia	fortiōrēs	fortiōra
Ab. fortibus		ācribus		potentibus		fortiōribus	

---

² The plural follows the pattern of the singular except that it has the plural endings.

³ Present participles follow the declension of **po-tēns** except that they have **-e** in the ablative singular when used as genuine participles.

⁴ For **-īs** (acc. pl.) see Ch. 16.

⁵ For irregular **plūs** see Ch. 27.

PRONOUNS

Demonstrative

hic, *this*   ille, *that*

	M.	**F.**	**N.**	**M.**	**F.**	**N.**
Sg.						
N.	hic	haec	hoc	ille	illa	illud
G.	huius	huius	huius	illīus	illīus	illīus
D.	huic	huic	huic	illī	illī	illī
A.	hunc	hanc	hoc	illum	illam	illud
Ab.	hōc	hāc	hōc	illō	illā	illō
Pl.						
N.	hī	hae	haec	illī	illae	illa
G.	hōrum	hārum	hōrum	illōrum	illārum	illōrum
D.	hīs	hīs	hīs	illīs	illīs	illīs
A.	hōs	hās	haec	illōs	illās	illa
Ab.	hīs	hīs	hīs	illīs	illīs	illīs

Relative			**Interrogative**[6]		**Intensive**		
quī, *who, which*			quis, *who?*		ipse, *himself,* etc.		
M.	**F.**	**N.**	**M. & F.**	**N.**	**M.**	**F.**	**N.**
Sg.							
N. quī	quae	quod	quis	quid	ipse	ipsa	ipsum
G. cuius	cuius	cuius	cuius	cuius	ipsīus	ipsīus	ipsīus
D. cui	cui	cui	cui	cui	ipsī	ipsī	ipsī
A. quem	quam	quod	quem	quid	ipsum	ipsam	ipsum
Ab. quō	quā	quō	quō	quō	ipsō	ipsā	ipsō
Pl.							
N. quī	quae	quae	(Plural is same		ipsī	ipsae	ipsa
G. quōrum	quārum	quōrum	as that of		ipsōrum	ipsārum	ipsōrum
D. quibus	quibus	quibus	relative.)		ipsīs	ipsīs	ipsīs
A. quōs	quās	quae			ipsōs	ipsās	ipsa
Ab. quibus	quibus	quibus			ipsīs	ipsīs	ipsīs

---

[6] The interrogative adjective **quī? quae? quod?** meaning *what? which? what kind of?* has the same declension as that of the relative pronoun.

PRONOUNS
Demonstrative

is, *this, that, he, she, it*   idem, *the same*

	M.	F.	N.	M.	F.	N.
Sg.						
N.	is	ea	id	īdem	eadem	idem
G.	eius	eius	eius	eiusdem	eiusdem	eiusdem
D.	eī	eī	eī	eīdem	eīdem	eīdem
A.	eum	eam	id	eundem	eandem	idem
Ab.	eō	eā	eō	eōdem	eādem	eōdem
Pl.						
N.	eī, iī	eae	ea	eīdem, īdem	eaedem	eadem
G.	eōrum	eārum	eōrum	eōrundem	eārundem	eōrundem
D.	eīs, iīs	eīs, iīs	eīs, iīs	eīsdem[7]	eīsdem	eīsdem
A.	eōs	eās	ea	eōsdem	eāsdem	eadem
Ab.	eīs	eīs	eīs	eīsdem	eīsdem	eīsdem

Irregular Adjectives[8]   **Personal[9]**   **Reflexive[9]**
sōlus, *alone, only*   suī, *himself,*
                                                                                                                              herself, itself

	M.	F.	N.	ego, *I*	tū, *you*	
Sg.						
N.	sōlus	sōla	sōlum	ego	tū	———
G.	sōlīus	sōlīus	sōlīus	meī	tuī	suī[10]
D.	sōlī	sōlī	sōlī	mihi	tibi	sibi
A.	sōlum	sōlam	sōlum	mē	tē	sē[11]
Ab.	sōlō	sōlā	sōlō	mē	tē	sē[11]
Pl.						
N.	sōlī	sōlae	sōla	nōs	vōs	———
G.	sōlōrum	sōlārum	sōlōrum	{ nostrum / nostrī	{ vestrum / vestrī	suī
D.	sōlīs	sōlīs	sōlīs	nōbīs	vōbīs	sibi
A.	sōlōs	sōlās	sōla	nōs	vōs	sē[11]
Ab.	sōlīs	sōlīs	sōlīs	nōbīs	vōbīs	sē[11]

[7] Also **īsdem.**

[8] Similarly **ūnus, tōtus, ūllus, nūllus, alius, alter, uter, neuter** (see Ch. 9).

[9] All forms of the pronouns of the first and second persons except the nom. sg. and the nom. pl. may also be used as reflexive pronouns.

[10] These forms are reflexive only. The nonreflexive forms of the third person are supplied by **is, ea, id** (see Chs. 11, 13).

[11] The form **sēsē** is also frequently found.

COMPARISON OF ADJECTIVES

Positive	Comparative	Superlative
Regular		
longus, -a, -um (*long*)	longior, -ius	longissimus, -a, -um
fortis, -e (*brave*)	fortior, -ius	fortissimus, -a, -um
fēlīx, *gen.* fēlīcis, (*happy*)	fēlīcior, -ius	fēlīcissimus, -a, -um
sapiēns, *gen.* sapientis (*wise*)	sapientior, -ius	sapientissimus, -a, -um
facilis, -e (*easy*)	facilior, -ius	facillimus, -a, -um
līber, -era, -erum (*free*)	līberior, -ius	līberrimus, -a, -um
pulcher, -chra, -chrum (*beautiful*)	pulchrior, -ius	pulcherrimus, -a, -um
ācer, ācris, ācre (*keen*)	ācrior, -ius	ācerrimus, -a, -um
Irregular		
bonus, -a, -um (*good*)	melior, -ius	optimus, -a, -um
magnus, -a, -um (*large*)	maior, -ius	maximus, -a, -um
malus, -a, -um (*bad*)	peior, -ius	pessimus, -a, -um
multus, -a, -um (*much*)	—, plūs	plūrimus, -a, -um
parvus, -a, -um (*small*)	minor, minus	minimus, -a, -um
(prae, prō)	prior, -ius (*former*)	prīmus, -a, -um
superus, -a, -um (*that above*)	superior, -ius	summus (suprēmus), -a, -um

COMPARISON OF ADVERBS

Positive	Comparative	Superlative
Regular		
longē (*far*)	longius	longissimē
fortiter (*bravely*)	fortius	fortissimē
fēlīciter (*happily*)	fēlīcius	fēlīcissimē
sapienter (*wisely*)	sapientius	sapientissimē
facile (*easily*)	facilius	facillimē
līberē (*freely*)	līberius	līberrimē
pulchrē (*beautifully*)	pulchrius	pulcherrimē
ācriter (*keenly*)	ācrius	ācerrimē
Irregular		
bene (*well*)	melius	optimē
magnopere (*greatly*)	magis	maximē
male (*badly*)	peius	pessimē
multum (*much*)	plūs	plūrimum
parum (*little*)	minus	minimē
(prae, prō)	prius (*before*)	prīmum; prīmō
diū (*a long time*)	diūtius	diūtissimē

NUMERALS

Cardinals	Ordinals	Roman Numerals
1. ūnus, -a, -um	prīmus, -a, -um	I
2. duo, duae, duo	secundus, alter	II
3. trēs, tria	tertius	III
4. quattuor	quārtus	IIII; IV
5. quīnque	quīntus	V
6. sex	sextus	VI
7. septem	septimus	VII
8. octō	octāvus	VIII
9. novem	nōnus	VIIII; IX
10. decem	decimus	X
11. ūndecim	ūndecimus	XI
12. duodecim	duodecimus	XII
13. tredecim	tertius decimus	XIII
14. quattuordecim	quārtus decimus	XIIII; XIV
15. quīndecim	quīntus decimus	XV
16. sēdecim	sextus decimus	XVI
17. septendecim	septimus decimus	XVII
18. duodēvīgintī	duodēvīcēsimus	XVIII
19. ūndēvīgintī	ūndēvīcēsimus	XVIIII; XIX
20. vīgintī	vīcēsimus	XX
21. vīgintī ūnus, ūnus et vīgintī	vīcēsimus prīmus	XXI
30. trīgintā	trīcēsimus	XXX
40. quadrāgintā	quadrāgēsimus	XXXX, XL
50. quīnquāgintā	quīnquāgēsimus	L
60. sexāgintā	sexāgēsimus	LX
70. septuāgintā	septuāgēsimus	LXX
80. octōgintā	octōgēsimus	LXXX
90. nōnāgintā	nōnāgēsimus	LXXXX; XC
100. centum	centēsimus	C
101. centum ūnus	centēsimus prīmus	CI
200. ducentī, -ae, -a	duocentēsimus	CC
300. trecentī	trecentēsimus	CCC
400. quadringentī	quadringentēsimus	CCCC
500. quīngentī	quīngentēsimus	D
600. sescentī	sescentēsimus	DC
700. septingentī	septingentēsimus	DCC
800. octingentī	octingentēsimus	DCCC
900. nōngentī	nōngentēsimus	DCCCC
1000. mīlle	mīllēsimus	M
2000. duo mīlia	bis mīllēsimus	MM

Declension of Numerals

For the declension of **ūnus** see Ch. 9 or **sōlus** above.
For **duo, trēs,** and **mīlle** see Ch. 15.
The forms from **trecentī** through **nōngentī** are declined in the plural like **ducentī, -ae, -a.**
The ordinals are declined like **prīmus, -a, -um.**
The other forms are indeclinable.

CONJUGATIONS 1–4

Principal Parts

1*st:* laudō	laudāre	laudāvī	laudātum
2*nd:* moneō	monēre	monuī	monitum
3*rd:* agō	agere	ēgī	āctum
4*th:* audiō	audīre	audīvī	audītum
3*rd* (**-iō**): capiō	capere	cēpī	captum

Indicative Active

Present

laudō	moneō	agō	audiō	capiō
laudās	monēs	agis	audīs	capis
laudat	monet	agit	audit	capit
laudāmus	monēmus	agimus	audīmus	capimus
laudātis	monētis	agitis	audītis	capitis
laudant	monent	agunt	audiunt	capiunt

Imperfect

laudābam	monēbam	agēbam	audiēbam	capiēbam
laudābās	monēbās	agēbās	audiēbās	capiēbās
laudābat	monēbat	agēbat	audiēbat	capiēbat
laudābāmus	monēbāmus	agēbāmus	audiēbāmus	capiēbāmus
laudābātis	monēbātis	agēbātis	audiēbātis	capiēbātis
laudābant	monēbant	agēbant	audiēbant	capiēbant

Future

laudābō	monēbō	agam	audiam	capiam
laudābis	monēbis	agēs	audiēs	capiēs
laudābit	monēbit	aget	audiet	capiet
laudābimus	monēbimus	agēmus	audiēmus	capiēmus
laudābitis	monēbitis	agētis	audiētis	capiētis
laudābunt	monēbunt	agent	audient	capient

Perfect

laudāvī	monuī	ēgī	audīvī	cēpī
laudāvistī	monuistī	ēgistī	audīvistī	cēpistī
laudāvit	monuit	ēgit	audīvit	cēpit
laudāvimus	monuimus	ēgimus	audīvimus	cēpimus
laudāvistis	monuistis	ēgistis	audīvistis	cēpistis
laudāvērunt	monuērunt	ēgērunt	audīvērunt	cēpērunt

Pluperfect

laudāveram	monueram	ēgeram	audīveram	cēperam
laudāverās	monuerās	ēgerās	audīverās	cēperās
laudāverat	monuerat	ēgerat	audīverat	cēperat
laudāverāmus	monuerāmus	ēgerāmus	audīverāmus	cēperāmus
laudāverātis	monuerātis	ēgerātis	audīverātis	cēperātis
laudāverant	monuerant	ēgerant	audīverant	cēperant

Future Perfect

laudāverō	monuerō	ēgerō	audīverō	cēperō
laudāveris	monueris	ēgeris	audīveris	cēperis
laudāverit	monuerit	ēgerit	audīverit	cēperit
laudāverimus	monuerimus	ēgerimus	audīverimus	cēperimus
laudāveritis	monueritis	ēgeritis	audīveritis	cēperitis
laudāverint	monuerint	ēgerint	audīverint	cēperint

Subjunctive Active

Present

laudem	moneam	agam	audiam	capiam
laudēs	moneās	agās	audiās	capiās
laudet	moneat	agat	audiat	capiat
laudēmus	moneāmus	agāmus	audiāmus	capiāmus
laudētis	moneātis	agātis	audiātis	capiātis
laudent	moneant	agant	audiant	capiant

Imperfect

laudārem	monērem	agerem	audīrem	caperem
laudārēs	monērēs	agerēs	audīrēs	caperēs
laudāret	monēret	ageret	audīret	caperet
laudārēmus	monērēmus	agerēmus	audīrēmus	caperēmus
laudārētis	monērētis	agerētis	audīrētis	caperētis
laudārent	monērent	agerent	audīrent	caperent

Perfect

laudāverim	monuerim	ēgerim	audīverim	cēperim
laudāverīs	monuerīs	ēgerīs	audīverīs	cēperīs
laudāverit	monuerit	ēgerit	audīverit	cēperit
laudāverīmus	monuerīmus	ēgerīmus	audīverīmus	cēperīmus
laudāverītis	monuerītis	ēgerītis	audīverītis	cēperītis
laudāverint	monuerint	ēgerint	audīverint	cēperint

Pluperfect

laudāvissem	monuissem	ēgissem	audīvissem	cēpissem
laudāvissēs	monuissēs	ēgissēs	audīvissēs	cēpissēs
laudāvisset	monuisset	ēgisset	audīvisset	cēpisset
laudāvissēmus	monuissēmus	ēgissēmus	audīvissēmus	cēpissēmus
laudāvissētis	monuissētis	ēgissētis	audīvissētis	cēpissētis
laudāvissent	monuissent	ēgissent	audīvissent	cēpissent

Present Imperative Active

laudā	monē	age	audī	cape
laudāte	monēte	agite	audīte	capite

Indicative Passive

Present

laudor	moneor	agor	audior	capior
laudāris(-re)	monēris(-re)	ageris(-re)	audīris(-re)	caperis(-re)
laudātur	monētur	agitur	audītur	capitur
laudāmur	monēmur	agimur	audīmur	capimur
laudāminī	monēminī	agiminī	audīminī	capiminī
laudantur	monentur	aguntur	audiuntur	capiuntur

Imperfect

laudābar	monēbar	agēbar	audiēbar	capiēbar
laudābāris(-re)	monēbāris(-re)	agēbāris(-re)	audiēbāris(-re)	capiēbāris(-re)
laudābātur	monēbātur	agēbātur	audiēbātur	capiēbātur
laudābāmur	monēbāmur	agēbāmur	audiēbāmur	capiēbāmur
laudābāminī	monēbāminī	agēbāminī	audiēbāminī	capiēbāminī
laudābantur	monēbantur	agēbantur	audiēbantur	capiēbantur

Future

laudābor	monēbor	agar	audiar	capiar
laudāberis(-re)	monēberis(-re)	agēris(-re)	audiēris(-re)	capiēris(-re)
laudābitur	monēbitur	agētur	audiētur	capiētur
laudābimur	monēbimur	agēmur	audiēmur	capiēmur
laudābiminī	monēbiminī	agēminī	audiēminī	capiēminī
laudābuntur	monēbuntur	agentur	audientur	capientur

Perfect

laudātus[12] sum	monitus sum	āctus sum	audītus sum	captus sum
laudātus es	monitus es	āctus es	audītus es	captus es
laudātus est	monitus est	āctus est	audītus est	captus est
laudātī sumus	monitī sumus	āctī sumus	audītī sumus	captī sumus
laudātī estis	monitī estis	āctī estis	audītī estis	captī estis
laudātī sunt	monitī sunt	āctī sunt	audītī sunt	captī sunt

Pluperfect

laudātus eram	monitus eram	āctus eram	audītus eram	captus eram
laudātus erās	monitus erās	āctus erās	audītus erās	captus erās
laudātus erat	monitus erat	āctus erat	audītus erat	captus erat
laudātī erāmus	monitī erāmus	āctī erāmus	audītī erāmus	captī erāmus
laudātī erātis	monitī erātis	āctī erātis	audītī erātis	captī erātis
laudātī erant	monitī erant	āctī erant	audītī erant	captī erant

Future Perfect

laudātus erō	monitus erō	āctus erō	audītus erō	captus erō
laudātus eris	monitus eris	āctus eris	audītus eris	captus eris
laudātus erit	monitus erit	āctus erit	audītus erit	captus erit
laudātī erimus	monitī erimus	āctī erimus	audītī erimus	captī erimus
laudātī eritis	monitī eritis	āctī eritis	audītī eritis	captī eritis
laudātī erunt	monitī erunt	āctī erunt	audītī erunt	captī erunt

Subjunctive Passive

Present

lauder	monear	agar	audiar	capiar
laudēris(-re)	moneāris(-re)	agāris(-re)	audiāris(-re)	capiāris(-re)
laudētur	moneātur	agātur	audiātur	capiātur
laudēmur	moneāmur	agāmur	audiāmur	capiāmur
laudēminī	moneāminī	agāminī	audiāminī	capiāminī
laudentur	moneantur	agantur	audiantur	capiantur

Imperfect

laudārer	monērer	agerer	audīrer	caperer
laudārēris(-re)	monērēris(-re)	agerēris(-re)	audīrēris(-re)	caperēris(-re)
laudārētur	monērētur	agerētur	audīrētur	caperētur
laudārēmur	monērēmur	agerēmur	audīrēmur	caperēmur
laudārēminī	monērēminī	agerēminī	audīrēminī	caperēminī
laudārentur	monērentur	agerentur	audīrentur	caperentur

---

[12] The participles **laudātus (-a, -um)**, **monitus (-a, -um)**, etc., are used as predicate adjectives, and so their endings vary to agree with the subject.

Perfect

laudātus sim	monitus sim	āctus sim	audītus sim	captus sim
laudātus sīs	monitus sīs	āctus sīs	audītus sīs	captus sīs
laudātus sit	monitus sit	āctus sit	audītus sit	captus sit
laudātī sīmus	monitī sīmus	āctī sīmus	audītī sīmus	captī sīmus
laudātī sītis	monitī sītis	āctī sītis	audītī sītis	captī sītis
laudātī sint	monitī sint	āctī sint	audītī sint	captī sint

Pluperfect

laudātus essem	monitus essem	āctus essem	audītus essem	captus essem
laudātus essēs	monitus essēs	āctus essēs	audītus essēs	captus essēs
laudātus esset	monitus esset	āctus esset	audītus esset	captus esset
laudātī essēmus	monitī essēmus	āctī essēmus	audītī essēmus	captī essēmus
laudātī essētis	monitī essētis	āctī essētis	audītī essētis	captī essētis
laudātī essent	monitī essent	āctī essent	audītī essent	captī essent

Present Imperative Passive

In classical Latin, passive form imperatives are found chiefly in deponent verbs (for forms, see Ch. 34).

Participles

Active

Pres.	laudāns	monēns	agēns	audiēns	capiēns
Fut.	laudātūrus	monitūrus	āctūrus	audītūrus	captūrus

Passive

Perf.	laudātus	monitus	āctus	audītus	captus
Fut.	laudandus	monendus	agendus	audiendus	capiendus

Infinitives

Active

Pres.	laudāre	monēre	agere	audīre	capere
Perf.	laudāvisse	monuisse	ēgisse	audīvisse	cēpisse
Fut.	laudātūrus esse	monitūrus esse	āctūrus esse	audītūrus esse	captūrus esse

Passive

Pres.	laudārī	monērī	agī	audīrī	capī
Perf.	laudātus esse	monitus esse	āctus esse	audītus esse	captus esse
Fut.	laudātum īrī	monitum īrī	āctum īrī	audītum īrī	captum īrī

DEPONENT VERBS

Principal Parts

1st Conj.:	hortor	hortārī	hortātus sum (*urge*)
2nd Conj.:	fateor	fatērī	fassus sum (*confess*)
3rd Conj.:	sequor	sequī	secūtus sum (*follow*)
4th Conj.:	mōlior	mōlīrī	mōlītus sum (*work at*)
3rd (-iō):	patior	patī	passus sum (*suffer*)

Indicative

Present

hortor	fateor	sequor	mōlior	patior
hortāris(-re)	fatēris(-re)	sequeris(-re)	mōlīris(-re)	pateris(-re)
hortātur	fatētur	sequitur	mōlītur	patitur
hortāmur	fatēmur	sequimur	mōlīmur	patimur
hortāminī	fatēminī	sequiminī	mōlīminī	patiminī
hortantur	fatentur	sequuntur	mōliuntur	patiuntur

Imperfect

hortābar	fatēbar	sequēbar	mōliēbar	patiēbar
hortābāris(-re)	fatēbāris(-re)	sequēbāris(-re)	mōliēbāris(-re)	patiēbāris(-re)
hortābātur	fatēbātur	sequēbātur	mōliēbātur	patiēbātur
hortābāmur	fatēbāmur	sequēbāmur	mōliēbāmur	patiēbāmur
hortābāminī	fatēbāminī	sequēbāminī	mōliēbāminī	patiēbāminī
hortābantur	fatēbantur	sequēbantur	mōliēbantur	patiēbantur

Future

hortābor	fatēbor	sequar	mōliar	patiar
hortāberis(-re)	fatēberis(-re)	sequēris(-re)	mōliēris(-re)	patiēris(-re)
hortābitur	fatēbitur	sequētur	mōliētur	patiētur
hortābimur	fatēbimur	sequēmur	mōliēmur	patiēmur
hortābiminī	fatēbiminī	sequēminī	mōliēminī	patiēminī
hortābuntur	fatēbuntur	sequentur	mōlientur	patientur

Perfect

hortātus sum	fassus sum	secūtus sum	mōlītus sum	passus sum
hortātus es	fassus es	secūtus es	mōlītus es	passus es
hortātus est	fassus est	secūtus est	mōlītus est	passus est
hortātī sumus	fassī sumus	secūtī sumus	mōlītī sumus	passī sumus
hortātī estis	fassī estis	secūtī estis	mōlītī estis	passī estis
hortātī sunt	fassī sunt	secūtī sunt	mōlītī sunt	passī sunt

Pluperfect

hortātus eram	fassus eram	secūtus eram	mōlītus eram	passus eram
hortātus erās	fassus erās	secūtus erās	mōlītus erās	passus erās
hortātus erat	fassus erat	secūtus erat	mōlītus erat	passus erat
hortātī erāmus	fassī erāmus	secūtī erāmus	mōlītī erāmus	passī erāmus
hortātī erātis	fassī erātis	secūtī erātis	mōlītī erātis	passī erātis
hortātī erant	fassī erant	secūtī erant	mōlītī erant	passī erant

Future Perfect

hortātus erō	fassus erō	secūtus erō	mōlītus erō	passus erō
hortātus eris	fassus eris	secūtus eris	mōlītus eris	passus eris
hortātus erit	fassus erit	secūtus erit	mōlītus erit	passus erit
hortātī erimus	fassī erimus	secūtī erimus	mōlītī erimus	passī erimus
hortātī eritis	fassī eritis	secūtī eritis	mōlītī eritis	passī eritis
hortātī erunt	fassī erunt	secūtī erunt	mōlītī erunt	passī erunt

Subjunctive

Present

horter	fatear	sequar	mōliar	patiar
hortēris(-re)	fateāris(-re)	sequāris(-re)	mōliāris(-re)	patiāris(-re)
hortētur	fateātur	sequātur	mōliātur	patiātur
hortēmur	fateāmur	sequāmur	mōliāmur	patiāmur
hortēminī	fateāminī	sequāminī	mōliāminī	patiāminī
hortentur	fateantur	sequantur	mōliantur	patiantur

Imperfect

hortārer	fatērer	sequerer	mōlīrer	paterer
hortārēris(-re)	fatērēris(-re)	sequerēris(-re)	mōlīrēris(-re)	paterēris(-re)
hortārētur	fatērētur	sequerētur	mōlīrētur	paterētur
hortārēmur	fatērēmur	sequerēmur	mōlīrēmur	paterēmur
hortārēminī	fatērēminī	sequerēminī	mōlīrēminī	paterēminī
hortārentur	fatērentur	sequerentur	mōlīrentur	paterentur

Perfect

hortātus sim	fassus sim	secūtus sim	mōlītus sim	passus sim
hortātus sīs	fassus sīs	secūtus sīs	mōlītus sīs	passus sīs
hortātus sit	fassus sit	secūtus sit	mōlītus sit	passus sit
hortātī sīmus	fassī sīmus	secūtī sīmus	mōlītī sīmus	passī sīmus
hortātī sītis	fassī sītis	secūtī sītis	mōlītī sītis	passī sītis
hortātī sint	fassī sint	secūtī sint	mōlītī sint	passī sint

Pluperfect

hortātus essem	fassus essem	secūtus essem	mōlītus essem	passus essem
hortātus essēs	fassus essēs	secūtus essēs	mōlītus essēs	passus essēs
hortātus esset	fassus esset	secūtus esset	mōlītus esset	passus esset
hortātī essēmus	fassī essēmus	secūtī essēmus	mōlītī essēmus	passī essēmus
hortātī essētis	fassī essētis	secūtī essētis	mōlītī essētis	passī essētis
hortātī essent	fassī essent	secūtī essent	mōlītī essent	passī essent

Present Imperative

hortāre	fatēre	sequere	mōlīre	patere
hortāminī	fatēminī	sequiminī	mōlīminī	patiminī

Participles

Pres.	hortāns	fatēns	sequēns	mōliēns	patiēns
Perf.	hortātus	fassus	secūtus	mōlītus	passus
Fut.	hortātūrus	fassūrus	secūtūrus	mōlītūrus	passūrus
Ger.	hortandus	fatendus	sequendus	mōliendus	patiendus

Infinitives

Pres.	hortārī	fatērī	sequī	mōlīrī	patī
Perf.	hortātus esse	fassus esse	secūtus esse	mōlītus esse	passus esse
Fut.	hortātūrus esse	fassūrus esse	secūtūrus esse	mōlītūrus esse	passūrus esse

IRREGULAR VERBS

Principal Parts

sum	esse	fuī	futūrum	(*be*)
possum	posse	potuī		(*be able, can*)
volō	velle	voluī		(*wish, be willing*)
nōlō	nōlle	nōluī		(*not to wish, be unwilling*)
mālō	mālle	māluī		(*prefer*)
eō	īre	iī	itum	(*go*)

Indicative[13]

Present

sum	possum	volō	nōlō	mālō	eō
es	potes	vīs	nōn vīs	māvīs	īs
est	potest	vult	nōn vult	māvult	it
sumus	possumus	volumus	nōlumus	mālumus	īmus
estis	potestis	vultis	nōn vultis	māvultis	ītis
sunt	possunt	volunt	nōlunt	mālunt	eunt

Imperfect

eram	poteram	volēbam	nōlēbam	mālēbam	ībam
erās	poterās	volēbās	nōlēbās	mālēbās	ībās
erat	poterat	volēbat	nōlēbat	mālēbat	ībat
erāmus	poterāmus	volēbāmus	nōlēbāmus	mālēbāmus	ībāmus
erātis	poterātis	volēbātis	nōlēbātis	mālēbātis	ībātis
erant	poterant	volēbant	nōlēbant	mālēbant	ībant

Future

erō	poterō	volam	nōlam	mālam	ībō
eris	poteris	volēs	nōlēs	mālēs	ībis
erit	poterit	volet	nōlet	mālet	ībit
erimus	poterimus	volēmus	nōlēmus	mālēmus	ībimus
eritis	poteritis	volētis	nōlētis	mālētis	ībitis
erunt	poterunt	volent	nōlent	mālent	ībunt

Perfect

fuī	potuī	voluī	nōluī	māluī	iī
fuistī	potuistī	voluistī	nōluistī	māluistī	īstī
fuit	potuit	voluit	nōluit	māluit	iit
fuimus	potuimus	voluimus	nōluimus	māluimus	iimus
fuistis	potuistis	voluistis	nōluistis	māluistis	īstis
fuērunt	potuērunt	voluērunt	nōluērunt	māluērunt	iērunt

Pluperfect

fueram	potueram	volueram	nōlueram	mālueram	ieram
fuerās	potuerās	voluerās	nōluerās	māluerās	ierās
etc.	etc.	etc.	etc.	etc.	etc.

Future Perfect

fuerō	potuerō	voluerō	nōluerō	māluerō	ierō
fueris	potueris	volueris	nōlueris	mālueris	ieris
etc.	etc.	etc.	etc.	etc.	etc.

Subjunctive

Present

sim	possim	velim	nōlim	mālim	eam
sīs	possīs	velīs	nōlīs	mālīs	eās
sit	possit	velit	nōlit	mālit	eat
sīmus	possīmus	velīmus	nōlīmus	mālīmus	eāmus
sītis	possītis	velītis	nōlītis	mālītis	eātis
sint	possint	velint	nōlint	mālint	eant

[13] Note that the verbs in this list have no passive voice (except for the idiomatic impersonal passive of **eō,** which is not used in this book).

Imperfect

essem	possem	vellem	nōllem	māllem	īrem
essēs	possēs	vellēs	nōllēs	māllēs	īrēs
esset	posset	vellet	nōllet	māllet	īret
essēmus	possēmus	vellēmus	nōllēmus	māllēmus	īrēmus
essētis	possētis	vellētis	nōllētis	māllētis	īrētis
essent	possent	vellent	nōllent	māllent	īrent

Perfect

fuerim	potuerim	voluerim	nōluerim	māluerim	ierim
fuerīs	potuerīs	voluerīs	nōluerīs	māluerīs	ierīs
fuerit	potuerit	voluerit	nōluerit	māluerit	ierit
fuerīmus	potuerīmus	voluerīmus	nōluerīmus	māluerīmus	ierīmus
fuerītis	potuerītis	voluerītis	nōluerītis	māluerītis	ierītis
fuerint	potuerint	voluerint	nōluerint	māluerint	ierint

Pluperfect

fuissem	potuissem	voluissem	nōluissem	māluissem	īssem
fuissēs	potuissēs	voluissēs	nōluissēs	māluissēs	īssēs
fuisset	potuisset	voluisset	nōluisset	māluisset	īsset
fuissēmus	potuissēmus	voluissēmus	nōluissēmus	māluissēmus	īssēmus
fuissētis	potuissētis	voluissētis	nōluissētis	māluissētis	īssētis
fuissent	potuissent	voluissent	nōluissent	māluissent	īssent

Present Imperative

es	———	———	nōlī	———	ī
este	———	———	nōlīte	———	īte

Participles

Pres. ———	potēns	volēns	nōlēns	———	iēns (*gen.* euntis)
Perf. ———	———	———	———	———	itum
Fut. futūrus	———	———	———	———	itūrus
Ger. ———	———	———	———	———	eundus

Infinitives

Pr. esse	posse	velle	nōlle	mālle	īre
Pf. fuisse	potuisse	voluisse	nōluisse	māluisse	īsse
Fu. futūrus esse *or* fore	———	———	———	———	itūrus esse

IRREGULAR: ferō, ferre, tulī, lātum, *to bear, carry*

Indicative

Present		Imperfect		Future	
Act.	**Pass.**	**Act.**	**Pass.**	**Act.**	**Pass.**
ferō	feror	ferēbam	ferēbar	feram	ferar
fers	ferris(-re)	ferēbās	ferēbāris(-re)	ferēs	ferēris(-re)
fert	fertur	ferēbat	ferēbātur	feret	ferētur
ferimus	ferimur	ferēbāmus	ferēbāmur	ferēmus	ferēmur
fertis	feriminī	ferēbātis	ferēbāminī	ferētis	ferēminī
ferunt	feruntur	ferēbant	ferēbantur	ferent	ferentur

Perfect Act.	Pass.	Pluperfect Act.	Pass.	Future Perfect Act.	Pass.
tulī	lātus sum	tuleram	lātus eram	tulerō	lātus erō
tulistī	lātus es	tulerās	lātus erās	tuleris	lātus eris
tulit	lātus est	tulerat	lātus erat	tulerit	lātus erit
etc.	etc.	etc.	etc.	etc.	etc.

Subjunctive

Present Act.	Pass.	Imperfect Act.	Pass.	Perfect Act.	Pass.
feram	ferar	ferrem	ferrer	tulerim	lātus sim
ferās	ferāris(-re)	ferrēs	ferrēris(-re)	tulerīs	lātus sīs
ferat	ferātur	ferret	ferrētur	tulerit	lātus sit
ferāmus	ferāmur	ferrēmus	ferrēmur	etc.	etc.
ferātis	ferāminī	ferrētis	ferrēminī		
ferant	ferantur	ferrent	ferrentur		

				Pluperfect	
				tulissem	lātus essem
				tulissēs	lātus essēs
				tulisset	lātus esset
				etc.	etc.

Pres. Imper. Act.	Pass.	Participles Act.	Pass.	Infinitives Act.	Pass.
fer	———	*Pres.* ferēns	———	ferre	ferrī
ferte	———	*Perf.* ———	lātus	tulisse	lātus esse
		Fut. lātūrus	ferendus	lātūrus esse	lātum īrī

IRREGULAR: fīō, fierī, factus sum, to happen, become; be made, be done

Indicative

Pres.	Impf.	Fut.	Perf.	Pluperf.	Fut. Perf.
fīō	fīēbam	fīam	factus sum	factus eram	factus erō
fīs	fīēbās	fīēs	factus es	factus erās	factus eris
fit	fīēbat	fīet	factus est	factus erat	factus erit
fīmus	fīēbāmus	fīēmus	factī sumus	factī erāmus	factī erimus
fītis	fīēbātis	fīētis	factī estis	factī erātis	factī eritis
fīunt	fīēbant	fīent	factī sunt	factī erant	factī erunt

Subjunctive

Pres.	Impf.	Perf.	Pluperf.
fīam	fierem	factus sim	factus essem
fīās	fierēs	factus sīs	factus essēs
fīat	fieret	factus sit	factus esset
fīāmus	fierēmus	factī sīmus	factī essēmus
fīātis	fierētis	factī sītis	factī essētis
fīant	fierent	factī sint	factī essent

Part.	Inf.
Pres. ———	fierī
Perf. factus	factus esse
Fut. faciendus	factum īrī

Imperative: fī, fīte

Wheelock Related Titles and Study Aids

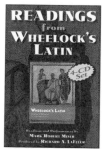

READINGS FROM WHEELOCK'S LATIN
Richard A. LaFleur and
Mark Robert Miner

A 4-CD audio package, converted to MP3, with recitation (in Restored Classical Pronunciation) of all vocabulary and paradigms for the 40 chapters of *Wheelock's Latin*.

The 4-CD package download features • Restored Classical Pronunciation • Vocabulary • Paradigms • *Sententiae Antiquae* • Narrative Passages • Selections from *Loci Antiqui*

Download, (318208kb) approximately 280 minutes, Prod. Code rwl

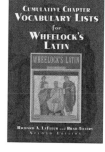

CUMULATIVE CHAPTER VOCABULARY LISTS FOR WHEELOCK'S LATIN
7th edition

Richard A. LaFleur and
Brad Tillery

Cumulative vocabulary lists for the 40 chapters of *Wheelock's Latin*. The list for each chapter contains all the words for that chapter as well as for all chapters preceding.

Features: • An invaluable study and review aid • Helpful for teachers in designing tests and in-class drills • Forty cumulative lists, hole punched and: • arranged by chapter of *Wheelock's Latin* • sorted by part of speech • nouns and verbs also sorted by declension/conjugation • including all English meanings, macrons, and accents

Shrink-wrapped, hole-punched 8 ½ x 11" pages, ISBN 978-0-86516-770-4

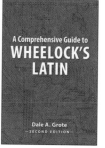

WHEELOCK'S LATIN GRAMMARQUICK
Richard A. LaFleur and
Brad Tillery

A quick and complete overview of Latin grammar—both forms and usage—on six durably laminated, double-sided cards, three-hole punched for easy insertion into notebooks. Arranged by part of speech, with summaries of all forms and the most common syntax, including case uses and subjunctive clauses. An essential homework/study/review companion to *Wheelock's Latin* and all introductory texts, and a handy reference guide for intermediate and more advanced students as well.

6 pages, (2007) Cardstock
ISBN 978-0-86516-666-0

38 LATIN STORIES
Anne H. Groton and James M. May

Originally designed as a supplement to the Latin course by F. M. Wheelock, this book is well suited for use in any introductory course, or as a quick-review course for 3rd semester.

vi + 104 pp. (5th edition, 1995) Paperback, ISBN 978-0-86516-289-1

A Tried and True Escort through Wheelock

A COMPREHENSIVE GUIDE TO WHEELOCK'S LATIN
Dale A. Grote

A study guide to accompany the current edition of *Wheelock's Latin*. This guide expands and explains important grammatical concepts that the Wheelock text presents too briefly for many contemporary students.

xix + 307 pp. (2003, new 6" x 9" size) Paperback, ISBN 978-0-86516-486-4

For all *"things"* Wheelock visit:
www.wheelockslatin.com

Bolchazy-Carducci Publishers, Inc. • www.bolchazy.com

Card Storagebox Bottom 1

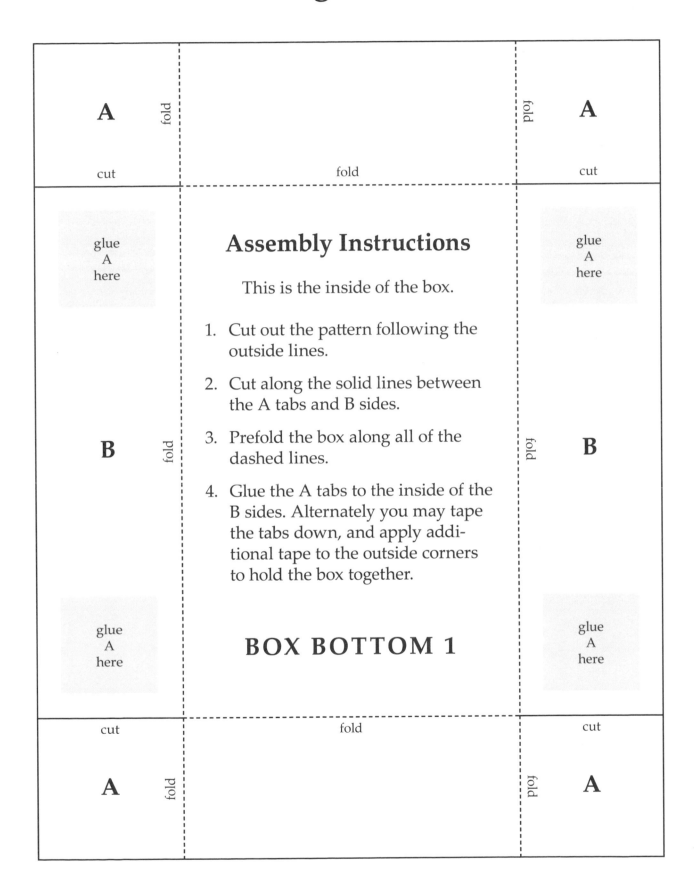

A

fold

fold

A

cut

fold

cut

glue
A
here

glue
A
here

Assembly Instructions

This is the inside of the box.

1. Cut out the pattern following the outside lines.

2. Cut along the solid lines between the A tabs and B sides.

3. Prefold the box along all of the dashed lines.

4. Glue the A tabs to the inside of the B sides. Alternately you may tape the tabs down, and apply additional tape to the outside corners to hold the box together.

B

fold

fold

B

glue
A
here

glue
A
here

BOX BOTTOM 1

cut

fold

cut

A

fold

fold

A

VOCABULARY CARDS AND GRAMMATICAL FORMS SUMMARY FOR WHEELOCK'S LATIN™

By Richard A. LaFleur and Brad Tillery

This indispensable study aid contains nearly 900 cards, arranged chapter-by-chapter to accompany all 40 chapters of WHEELOCK'S LATIN, each with full, unabbreviated Latin vocabulary entry, chapter number, and card number on one side, and English meanings and derivatives or cognates on the reverse side. Also included are: an alphabetical list of all words with their card numbers; suggestions on vocabulary study and use of the cards; and a handy Summary of Forms for grammar review.

These cards are for use with WHEELOCK'S LATIN, by Frederic M. Wheelock and revised by Richard A. LaFleur.

™Wheelock's Latin, copyright by Martha Wheelock, Deborah Wheelock Taylor, and Richard A. LaFleur. "WHEELOCK'S" is a trademark of Martha Wheelock and Deborah Wheelock Taylor. Wheelock's Latin, by Frederic M. Wheelock and revised by Richard A. LaFleur, is available through your local bookstore or online at www.harpercollins.com.

Bolchazy-Carducci Publishers, Inc.
1570 Baskin Road, Mundelein, IL 60060
Phone: (847) 526-4344; Fax: (847) 526-2867
www.bolchazy.com

Card Storagebox Bottom 2

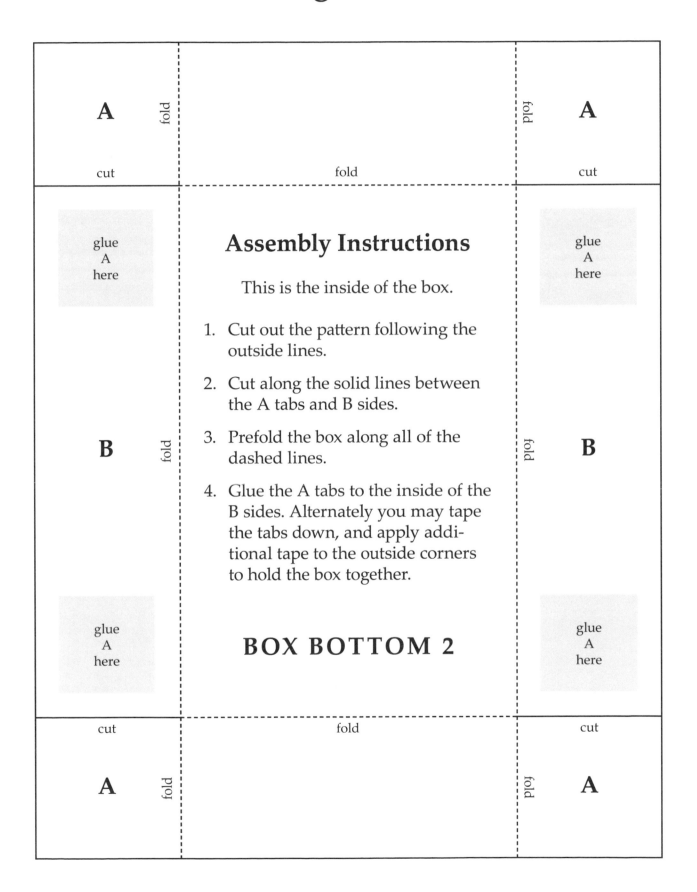

A

fold

fold

A

cut

fold

cut

glue A here

glue A here

Assembly Instructions

This is the inside of the box.

1. Cut out the pattern following the outside lines.

2. Cut along the solid lines between the A tabs and B sides.

3. Prefold the box along all of the dashed lines.

4. Glue the A tabs to the inside of the B sides. Alternately you may tape the tabs down, and apply additional tape to the outside corners to hold the box together.

BOX BOTTOM 2

B

fold

B

glue A here

glue A here

cut

fold

cut

A

fold

fold

A

VOCABULARY CARDS AND GRAMMATICAL FORMS SUMMARY FOR WHEELOCK'S LATIN™

By Richard A. LaFleur and Brad Tillery

This indispensable study aid contains nearly 900 cards, arranged chapter-by-chapter to accompany all 40 chapters of WHEELOCK'S LATIN, each with full, unabbreviated Latin vocabulary entry, chapter number, and card number on one side, and English meanings and derivatives or cognates on the reverse side. Also included are: an alphabetical list of all words with their card numbers; suggestions on vocabulary study and use of the cards; and a handy Summary of Forms for grammar review.

These cards are for use with WHEELOCK'S LATIN, by Frederic M. Wheelock and revised by Richard A. LaFleur.

Bolchazy-Carducci Publishers, Inc.
1570 Baskin Road, Mundelein, IL 60060
Phone: (847) 526-4344; Fax: (847) 526-2867
www.bolchazy.com